Jesus said, 'I am'

The Bible Reading Fellowship
15 The Chambers, Vineyard
Abingdon OX14 3FE
brf.org.uk

The Bible Reading Fellowship (BRF) is a Registered Charity (233280)

ISBN 978 0 85746 562 7
First published 2019
10 9 8 7 6 5 4 3 2 1 0

Acknowledgements
Unless otherwise acknowledged, scripture quotations are from The New Revised Standard Version of the Bible, Anglicised edition, copyright © 1989, 1995 by the Division of Christian Education of the National Council of the Churches of Christ in the United States of America. Used by permission. All rights reserved.

Scripture taken from the New Century Version®. Copyright © 2005 by Thomas Nelson. Used by permission. All rights reserved.

Scripture quotations taken from the Holy Bible, English Standard Version, published by HarperCollins Publishers, © 2001 Crossway Bibles, a division of Good News Publishers. Used by permission. All rights reserved.

Scripture quotations taken from The Holy Bible, New International Version (Anglicised edition) copyright © 1979, 1984, 2011 by Biblica. Used by permission of Hodder & Stoughton Publishers, a Hachette UK company. All rights reserved. 'NIV' is a registered trademark of Biblica. UK trademark number 1448790.

Every effort has been made to trace and contact copyright owners for material used in this resource. We apologise for any inadvertent omissions or errors, and would ask those concerned to contact us so that full acknowledgement can be made in the future.

A catalogue record for this book is available from the British Library

Printed and bound by CPI Group (UK) Ltd, Croydon CR0 4YY

Andrea Skevington

Jesus said, 'I am'

Finding life in the everyday

To the women of my Thursday afternoon group.
Thank you for your love and wisdom.
It is a privilege to walk with you.

To St John's, Woodbridge, especially those on
the Advent retreat, and the Otley Hall retreaters,
who graciously tried out early ideas for this book.
Your responses helped to shape it.

To the people of St Andrew's, Melton, for your kindness.

To Wells Cathedral, Norwich Cathedral and
St Mary's, Buscot, for inspiration and assistance.

Contents

Preface

Jesus said many startling, strange things, but few can match the 'I am' sayings for originality, for opening our eyes to see things differently. This book will begin to explore these sayings in John's gospel, with a particular aim in mind: to encourage us to find ways of living out Jesus' teaching in our daily lives. John says, 'We have seen his glory' (1:14) and, strangely, this glory shows itself in these simple examples from daily lived experience – bread, light, gates, shepherds, life, ways. In doing so, it sparks the imagination. These 'I am' sayings go deep, disclosing their truth slowly, little by little, as we can begin to accept it.

So, this book will explore the signs and stories that surround these 'I am' sayings of Jesus. We will look at what they might mean for us as we seek to deepen our understanding of Jesus and, perhaps, walk along his way.

It is an everyday grammatical necessity, saying 'I am' – *ego eimi* in Greek – and Jesus says it 24 times in John's account. Seven of these are usually called 'I am' sayings, and these form the core of the book. We will also give a chapter to the saying associated with the woman at the well, too interesting to overlook, as well as nodding to others. I believe each one of these has a claim to be considered part of John's great project of revealing who Jesus is, and that in him is abundant life.

Writing this book has changed the way I see following Jesus. My discipleship has become more fluid, more lived, more compassionate and outward looking. It is more grounded in relationship and service. The commands to love seem in sharper focus. I hope that, as you read it, you may go deeper into the adventure of discovering who Jesus is and who you are.

Each chapter is in two parts. The first half is an exploration of the saying and its context; the second is a selection of things you can do – 'reflection and response'. I have tried to make this as broad and varied as I can, hoping you will find something that draws you on a first reading, but also offers depth and breadth for a future reading. There are questions to take you deeper, and further reading if you want to explore the ideas more. There are prayer and meditation prompts, creative activities, suggestions for activities you can do with and in service of your community. Some of the ideas suggested are things I have done with small groups, in retreat settings or in informal church settings. Others are practices I follow myself. Many of the ideas could be used in newly imagined ways of doing church, for example the Fresh Expressions movement, or small informal groups that meet in houses, coffee shops, pubs or dance studios. Most of the active and reflective ideas could be used in all-age settings and services, in families and with children's or youth groups. I hope that nearly all the ideas can be used by one person, or more than one, as it suits your circumstances.

There is plenty of choice, so pick one thing that catches your attention and try it. If it suits you better, choose a section, and pick the first item, and just do that. I hope this book will provide you with resources for many years of exploring what it means to live out the words of Jesus. May it help you to walk in the light.

1

I am: Moses and Abraham

One day Moses was taking care of Jethro's flock... When Moses led the flock to the west side of the desert, he came to Sinai, the mountain of God. There the angel of the Lord appeared to him in flames of fire coming out of a bush. Moses saw that the bush was on fire, but it was not burning up. So he said, 'I will go closer to this strange thing. How can a bush continue burning without burning up?'

When the Lord saw that Moses was coming to look at the bush, God called to him from the bush, 'Moses, Moses!'

And Moses said, 'Here I am.'

Then God said, 'Do not come any closer. Take off your sandals, because you are standing on holy ground. I am the God of your ancestors – the God of Abraham, the God of Isaac, and the God of Jacob.' Moses covered his face because he was afraid to look at God.

The Lord said, 'I have seen the troubles my people have suffered in Egypt, and I have heard their cries when the Egyptian slave masters hurt them. I am concerned about their pain, and I have come down to save them from the Egyptians. I will bring them out of that land and lead them to a good land with lots of room – a fertile land. It is the land of the Canaanites, Hittites, Amorites, Perizzites, Hivites, and Jebusites. I have heard the cries of the people of Israel, and I have seen the way the Egyptians have made life hard for them. So now I am sending you to the king of Egypt. Go! Bring my people, the Israelites, out of Egypt!'

But Moses said to God, 'I am not a great man! How can I go to the king and lead the Israelites out of Egypt?'

> **God said, 'I will be with you. This will be the proof that I am sending you. After you lead the people out of Egypt, all of you will worship me on this mountain.'**
>
> **Moses said to God, 'When I go to the Israelites, I will say to them, "The God of your ancestors sent me to you." What if the people say, "What is his name?" What should I tell them?'**
>
> **Then God said to Moses, 'I am who I am. When you go to the people of Israel, tell them, "I am sent me to you."'**
>
> EXODUS 3:1–14 (NCV)

John's gospel looks back to Moses' ancient story, recording for us how Jesus called himself by this name – 'I am'. This name, which emerged from a burning bush so long ago, is one of the most identifiable features of John's account. It resonated with his early readers and listeners in Greek Ephesus, and it stirs our imagination even today, millennia later. Before we go deep into John's account, and explore why that may be, we will look back to Moses' story and see what we understand of this earliest 'I am'.

The story of Moses

At the moment when Moses first glimpses the burning bush, it is a story of failure: he had been at the centre of power and influence, and now was pushed beyond the margins. Moses went from being high in Pharaoh's court to a nomad shepherd, living in the wilderness. Moses – rescued from the Nile by Pharaoh's daughter, raised in the richest and most powerful household in the known world – killed an Egyptian slave master and was exiled. In exile, he again showed his acute sense of justice, defending Jethro's daughters. So, on his way down, he was involved in two rescues – one led to murder, the second to marriage. Even in his descent, there are signs of hope and growth.

The decades he spent in the wilderness, keeping Jethro's flocks, gave him time to learn what he needed to learn before bringing the ex-slaves through this same desert. There were practical things –

how to navigate, lead, find water, grazing and shelter from weather, and hide or fight predators. More importantly, there were matters of character. This is slow-growing fruit. He learned humility, among other things; after all, his high hopes had come to nothing. Perhaps he was learning some of the way described by Jesus so much later: the way of losing before you can find, of the first becoming last and the last, first (Matthew 16:25; 19:30).

Nothing is wasted in God's economy. God used the rubbish – and the good – in Moses' upbringing and his life as a shepherd. He became ideally suited to his task. As well as his circumstances and experience, God used his character; in this case, a sense of justice and an indignation at bullies. What must have felt like failure and a downwards path was the place where Moses encountered God.

We do not know if he was seeking God when God appeared. We do know that he was in the middle of his everyday, working life, and that God did something strange to arrest his attention, awaken his curiosity, draw him nearer. Attention and curiosity can guide you, can awaken you to God in the burning bushes we pass every day.

Moses certainly didn't seem to be looking for a job, let alone a great mission. It is easy to read his rather thin excuses and wonder why he spent so long arguing. His unwillingness to respond seems to come from uncertainty.

Who?

Moses is uncertain about himself, and he is uncertain about God.

His uncertainty about himself is understandable: plucked from death, set apart for great things, and then fallen, feared, unable to help his suffering people (Exodus 1—2). He has had a long time to tell himself this story – the story of one who missed his moment and squandered his opportunities, unable to fulfil his destiny. So when the moment came back to him, he did not know what to do with it.

Moses had lost his sense of his true nature. How did he respond to God's?

He is afraid to look on God – the God of people, his ancestors. It is interesting that God here chooses to be known by relationship – God could have spoken of being almighty, powerful, the Lord of hosts. Instead, God identifies as the one who has walked with people and has known people. It is a wonderful thing to be known for relationship like this: to be the God who is with us and for us. But it carries a risk: that people may go from thinking God is for them to thinking God is against others. There is a risk of exclusivity, superiority, built in the way flawed humans respond to the love of God. The great tragedy is that this is how the Israelites came to think at times, and how many tribes of believers have come to think even to the present day. Nevertheless, the story we have in the scriptures is one of gradually unfolding relationship, with people, communities, nations. This God is and will be a light for all (Revelation 21:23–24).

'I am': the name of God?

The God of ancestors is how God identifies himself. It is not enough for Moses; he wants more. Perhaps he knows he may be thought of as a traitor to his people – these ancestors – and wants the authority a specific name gives. And this is the name he is offered:

> I am what I am [or, 'I will be what I will be'].
> EXODUS 3:14

This is a God who is beyond naming. God just is, or maybe God is the ground of being. There is more here that we miss because we are reading a translation. There is a connection between the verb 'to be' and the letters of the word YHWH – usually translated as 'Lord' in English Bibles – one of the principal names for God in the Hebrew scriptures. The one who is, is Lord. And there is more: the sounding out of two syllables of YHWH is like a breath, in and out. It is the word of life itself. It is both beyond our naming and as intimate as breath. Later, Moses will be given a set of commandments for the people when they have left slavery (Exodus 20), and this is the third of the ten:

> You shall not make wrongful use of the name of the Lord your God, for the Lord will not acquit anyone who misuses his name.
> EXODUS 20:7

Names matter. Names have power. One interpretation of this command I have heard from a Jewish perspective is that anything we say about God will be at best incomplete, at worst wrong. God is beyond our language and more than we can know. To speak of God may lead to making a false image in our minds of what God is like. So, be humble in how you use the name. This 'I am' given to Moses is a name beyond names.

It balances the specificity of the previous name, 'the God of...' and makes us consider that this God is a God who has something to say to the Egyptians, too.

Two ways God identifies himself: as the God of individuals, walking alongside, knowing and loving people; and the God beyond our imagining, the God in whom we all live and move (Acts 17:28). The God of our every breath. Both. This is a mystery worth pondering.

But the conversation returns to the particular very rapidly.

So, go – you have a job to do.

'Who am I?' Moses asks (Exodus 3:11). That is the question – a very profound question. Who you are is less important than the presence of the God who is God of relationship, it seems. The answer is, 'I will be with you.'

And then, Moses asks for a sign. God's answer is a little unsatisfactory to Moses. The sign is that you will succeed. When you have brought the people out of Egypt, you will worship God on this mountain – this very mountain where the bush burns. You trust, you go, it works. This sign is no help in giving you confidence or certainty to step forward and do this hard thing. The sign is that you will look back when you have done it, and then you know that it really was God who was with you. Life often makes more sense when we read it backwards.

Eventually, when he gets to the point of believing and accepting God, Moses still does not believe or accept himself. It's as if he thinks God doesn't know who he's chosen. When Moses points out that he's not a good orator, God's reply suggests: 'I know very well what your limitations are. I still choose you.' God will give what is necessary for the job to be done. And once he finally leaves on this journey, he sees Aaron, his brother, whom he has not seen for many years, coming to meet him. Why did Aaron come to find his brother now, we wonder? This is the kind of sign that helps. God does not leave Moses alone. In this story with strange signs and wonders, with plagues and snakes and magicians, we have another example of apparently ordinary things, like reconciliation with a long-lost brother, transformed and illuminated with the glory of God.

'In the beginning was the Word'

John structured his gospel, his account of the life of Jesus, around this 'I am', this ancient and mysterious word for God. Why?

John starts his gospel (1:1–18) at the beginning, before anything was made, and places the Word, in Greek the *Logos*, there, with God – beyond understanding, beyond definition.

Then, this happens. The Word does not stay intangible:

> And the Word became flesh and lived among us, and we have seen his glory, the glory as of a father's only son, full of grace

> and truth... No one has ever seen God. It is God the only son, who is close to the Father's heart, who has made him known.
> JOHN 1:14, 18

We can see John's intention here: to show that this *Logos* and Jesus of Nazareth are the same: that Jesus is Christ, existing since the foundation of the world, and yet someone he has seen. In seeing Jesus, he says, we can see what God is like.

John uses the word 'Christ' twice in his gospel in his own voice, rather than in the speech of others: once in the first chapter (1:17), and once again when he is explaining that in believing, we may have life (20:31).

In between these two bold statements, he unfolds and develops the meaning in different ways. The idea needs to grow in our minds. It takes time for us to see it.

John is saying the mysterious unknowable *Logos* is embodied in the person he ate with and laughed with and wept with, whose mother he cared for in her grief. It is a bold task to attempt. The 'I am's are part of this process, ringing though John's account, inviting us to consider that Jesus is at one time this great 'I am', and also as tangible as bread, as a vine laden with grapes.

Before Abraham

We begin briefly, then, not with the first 'I am' saying, but possibly the strangest. Not drawing on natural world or symbol, but speaking to the religious leaders of his day directly and dramatically.

> Before Abraham was, I am.
> JOHN 8:58

What might it mean?

This extraordinary saying brings to an end a rather heated exchange, which began after Jesus sends away the woman caught in adultery (8:12). The religious leaders question his authority and freely claim the name and authority of Abraham. As he speaks, Jesus points to a closeness to God, a knowledge and a life within God, a life which is not confined to a human lifespan, which gives him precedence even over Abraham. As we read it, we remember what John said as he introduced us to the story of Jesus: 'He was in the beginning with God' (1:1–4). This 'I am' saying takes us into the territory of the mysterious burning bush most closely. It is an outrageous, blasphemous saying in the eyes of the religious leaders, and they pick up stones for him, as they did for the woman. They respond in anger, but Jesus slips away, for now, and the story continues.

As we read together, as we explore these sayings, we will come to see how other people responded to him. We will see too how he listened, how he fed, healed, encouraged and set people on their feet. We will follow him as he walks alongside the lost and despairing, and kneels before his friends. We will see one who is 'full of grace and truth' (1:14), and who was described as having words of life (6:68).

Reflection and response

Study

Exodus 3

- Do you think that the mountain was already regarded as holy, or did this encounter make it so (vv. 1, 5)?
- Are there places in which you find it easier to become aware of the presence of God? If so, what are they like?

- Consider the significance of the burning bush – on fire but not consumed. Has God caught your attention lately (vv. 2–4)? How did you respond (vv. 5–6)?
- Do you have a tradition of faith in your family? Is there a faith of your ancestors? Whether you do or not – what does that mean for you (v. 6)?
- How does God respond to his suffering people? What does he want to do, and how (vv. 7–10)?
- Why do you think Moses asks for a definite name for God (v. 13)?
- How do you tend to think of God – as 'I am', or as the God of people in your past, or some other way? What does God as 'I am' mean to you?

Further study

John 1:1–18

- In what ways do you think John draws on Genesis 1 to begin his gospel? Are there echoes, and words or ideas that are picked up? It is a strange way to begin a life story. Why might he have done it this way?
- What difference might it make to our view of creation to see it as described in verses 3–4?
- How does John speak of light and life? What connections do you see between the two ideas (vv. 4–5)?
- What expectations of the story of Jesus are being set up?
- Do you think there are ways we might miss recognising and receiving Jesus now (vv. 10–11)?
- What do you understand by Jesus coming from the Father and living among us (vv. 14, 16–18)?
- What do you think John meant when he said he had seen his glory (v. 14)?
- What kind of blessings/gifts do you think John meant here (v. 16–17)?
- What might it mean that Jesus makes God known (v. 18)?

Prayer and meditation

The God of Abraham

How do you respond to the idea that God can be the God of a person as well as a people? That Jesus makes God known to us? Find some quiet time, and open yourself to God in silent prayer, asking, if you can, to be aware of the presence of God. As distracting thoughts arrive, keep turning back to God. God wants to be known by direct experience.

Breath prayer

The Hebrew name for God, similar in sound to the Hebrew for 'I am', is also similar to the pattern of breath: YHWH. You might like to find another word, or a pair of words, to use as a breath prayer. Practise in times of calm; it may help in times of distress. Suggestions to breathe in and out:

- Love, Thanks
- Peace, Joy
- Good, Love

Prayer for liberation

Many things can hold us, and those we love, captive. Pray for yourself and others to be set free from fear, debt, mental and physical distress, addiction, patterns of wrongdoing, etc. Pray for those who work to set others free. Pray too for those caught up in modern slavery in various forms. Pray for liberation.

Creative response

Maps (Moses' story)

Remember that the events of Moses' life, both good and bad, were places on the road to this encounter and his task. When we look back at our past successes and failures, what do we see?

Reflect on your life – you might like to draw a map to represent your journey. You can connect it to real places, or symbolic ones like in Bunyan's *The Pilgrim's Progress* (1678). For this exercise, do you see good emerging in unexpected ways? It doesn't always, of course.

Alternatively, rewrite your own life's story, again focusing on real or symbolic places along the way.

Burning bush

> *Earth's crammed with heaven,*
> *And every common bush afire with God,*
> *But only he who sees, takes off his shoes.*
> Elizabeth Barrett Browning (1806–61)[1]

As you start your day, pray for open eyes to see where God may be at work, or may be seeking to catch your attention today. Set off with open eyes, a camera and a notepad. Record anything that draws your attention. At the end of the day, mull over what you have recorded in prayer. What did you see?

John's prologue: re-imagining

What particularly strikes you about John's prologue (John 1:1–18)? Stay with any words/images that catch your attention or puzzle you. Use pencils or paints to capture the movements and moods of this passage. You could engage in 'holy doodling' with the words and any shapes and patterns that emerge from them.

Alternatively, write a retelling, emphasising the aspects that caught your attention.

Life and service

God appeared to Moses to call him to lead his people. Are there ways God may be calling you to love and service?

Holy

God meets us and, where he does, it is holy ground. Can you see all ground as holy? Can you say that of the places and spaces you visit today? Pray over them. Then, if appropriate, mark the places in some way, with a temporary reminder.

Our abilities and our story

Think of how God used Moses' character and history to bring the people out of slavery. What about you – your character and history? Do you have abilities you are using, or could use? (Use the 'Maps' exercise from page 17 if you did it.)

You could ask people you trust to help you see your own talents, what you have to offer and what you are already doing. If you wish, consider going further.

Are there ways you can use your talents and experience for the benefit of others? Are there people you can walk alongside and encourage? Can you be generous with what you can do? Can even the really hard times enable you to help someone going through something similar? Even if you feel you have nothing, you have the capacity to listen with compassion, to encourage another, to say a prayer.

'From his fullness we have all received, grace upon grace' (John 1:16). Are there ways in which you could increasingly be part of passing on blessings?

Pray for God's kingdom to come.

Slavery and freedom

Moses was called to lead his people out of slavery. Research modern slavery, racism or discrimination. Consider ways you could be part of the solution – by prayer, campaigning, awareness, providing practical support for those affected, etc.

'Through him all things were made'

Spend time in the natural world, or bring pictures and objects in to where you are. Consider them, delight in them, as you remember the mystery of the Word through whom they were made.

Can you join in with the care of creation? Here are a few suggestions: growing things, providing homes for wildlife, buying local food, avoiding chemicals, reducing your carbon footprint, supporting campaigns to protect the environment.

Other creative ideas

There may be ways you can participate in this outpouring of creativity in any field. Consider ways in which you were creative as a child, which you have left behind: crafting, engaging with science and engineering, making and restoring, as well as more traditional arts. Which can you engage in to the glory of God?

Further reading

Shane Claiborne, *Jesus for President* (Zondervan, 2008)
Malcolm Guite, *Parable and Paradox* (Canterbury Press, 2016), especially the 'I am' sonnets
John Ortburg, *Soul Keeping* (Zondervan, 2014)
Barbara Brown Taylor, *An Altar in the World* (Canterbury Press, 2009)
Dallas Willard, *The Spirit of the Disciplines* (Harper, 1988)
Tom Wright, *John for Everyone* (SPCK, 2002)

Closing prayer

Lord,
We hope to see your glory, full of grace and truth.
We thank you that you are 'I am', you are our ground of being, as close as breath.
We give thanks that you are the one who walked with Moses to set the people free.
Thank you that, through Jesus, your nature is known to us.
Thank you that our everyday realities – a bush, a loaf of bread, a vine – can be signs of grace and truth.
Help us to be signs of your love and liberation where we are.
Help us to be people of the 'I am'.
Amen

2

The woman at the well

Now when Jesus learned that the Pharisees had heard that Jesus was making and baptising more disciples than John (although Jesus himself did not baptise, but only his disciples), he left Judea and departed again for Galilee. And he had to pass through Samaria. So he came to a town of Samaria called Sychar, near the field that Jacob had given to his son Joseph. Jacob's well was there; so Jesus, wearied as he was from his journey, was sitting beside the well. It was about the sixth hour.

A woman from Samaria came to draw water. Jesus said to her, 'Give me a drink.' (For his disciples had gone away into the city to buy food.) The Samaritan woman said to him, 'How is it that you, a Jew, ask for a drink from me, a woman of Samaria?' (For Jews have no dealings with Samaritans.) Jesus answered her, 'If you knew the gift of God, and who it is that is saying to you, 'Give me a drink', you would have asked him, and he would have given you living water.' The woman said to him, 'Sir, you have nothing to draw water with, and the well is deep. Where do you get that living water? Are you greater than our father Jacob? He gave us the well and drank from it himself, as did his sons and his livestock.' Jesus said to her, 'Everyone who drinks of this water will be thirsty again, but whoever drinks of the water that I will give him will never be thirsty again. The water that I will give him will become in him a spring of water welling up to eternal life.' The woman said to him, 'Sir, give me this water, so that I will not be thirsty or have to come here to draw water.'

Jesus said to her, 'Go, call your husband, and come here.'

The woman answered him, 'I have no husband.' Jesus said to her, 'You are right in saying, 'I have no husband'; for you have had five husbands, and the one you now have is not your husband. What you have said is true.' The woman said to him, 'Sir, I perceive that you are a prophet. Our fathers worshipped on this mountain, but you say that in Jerusalem is the place where people ought to worship.' Jesus said to her, 'Woman, believe me, the hour is coming when neither on this mountain nor in Jerusalem will you worship the Father. You worship what you do not know; we worship what we know, for salvation is from the Jews. But the hour is coming, and is now here, when the true worshippers will worship the Father in spirit and truth, for the Father is seeking such people to worship him. God is spirit, and those who worship him must worship in spirit and truth.' The woman said to him, 'I know that Messiah is coming (he who is called Christ). When he comes, he will tell us all things.' Jesus said to her, 'I who speak to you am he.'

Just then his disciples came back. They marvelled that he was talking with a woman, but no one said, 'What do you seek?' or, 'Why are you talking with her?' So the woman left her water jar and went away into town and said to the people, 'Come, see a man who told me all that I ever did. Can this be the Christ?' They went out of the town and were coming to him...

Many Samaritans from that town believed in him because of the woman's testimony, 'He told me all that I ever did.' So when the Samaritans came to him, they asked him to stay with them, and he stayed there two days. And many more believed because of his word. They said to the woman, 'It is no longer because of what you said that we believe, for we have heard for ourselves, and we know that this is indeed the Saviour of the world.'

JOHN 4:1–30, 39–42 (ESV)

This is a remarkable story, the longest conversation Jesus is recorded as having in any of the gospels. It is one of a pair, following on from

Jesus' deep conversation with Nicodemus. There, he talked to a wealthy, privileged, learned man at night. Here, he talks to a humble outsider, a woman, at noon. John records for us how Jesus speaks to these two people in ways they find hard to understand at first, but which are utterly compelling for them, drawing them into a whole new way of seeing and being. Although not one of the classic seven 'I am' sayings, I feel this passage is too important, too intriguing to overlook. It is the first time Jesus says 'I am', and by it he announces he is the Messiah, the Christ – to a Samaritan woman, outside Israel. It is a monumental moment, a bursting out of truth.

Conflict or common ground?

Jews avoided travelling through Samaria, which was hostile territory for them. Various translations speak of Jesus being compelled to travel this way, rather than the usual route skirting the edge. Perhaps he was compelled by the Spirit to meet this woman and her community.

Conflict seems to be the place this story begins – and not only the old conflict between the Jews and the Samaritans, with its roots in the Assyrian invasion many centuries before. There was more immediate potential conflict facing Jesus.

The Pharisees had been scorekeeping – counting how many disciples Jesus had compared with John. They were busy with their measuring sticks, setting up a potential for rivalry between John and Jesus. Such rivalry, such counting, could do untold damage. Jesus was more successful than John and was baptising more people, and so Jesus stepped out of the game to return to Galilee. I suspect that most of us would not walk away from success like this; most of us find a numbers game hard to resist. But Jesus walks away from the crowds, success, jealousy, envy and conflict such success could produce. Instead, he finds one woman, far away from the centres of power. To her, he talks of water – perhaps continuing the line of thought he shared with Nicodemus – of baptism and spirit, and of water that gives life. It does not seem a good move to pass through Samaria. Is Jesus escaping one lot of conflict and rivalry, only to land in another?

Jesus stops to rest near the plot of ground that Jacob gave his son Joseph. Jacob's other name was Israel – one who wrestles with God. We are going back to a common spring, a common source, at Jacob's well. We are being reminded of a time before the kingdom was divided and the Jews and Samaritans became separate peoples. We remember Joseph's role in the whole story, and how his bones were carried out of the land with Moses and buried in this place. It is ground that holds meaning and memory for Jews and Samaritans – of their common father and their common salvation story of slavery and exodus and freedom.

Against a setting of conflict, we see Jesus acting out his mission to be a peacemaker, a reconciler: 'For he is our peace; in his flesh he has made both groups into one and has broken down the dividing wall, that is, the hostility between us,' as Paul writes in Ephesians 2:14. Jesus himself is common ground. As we look at how we are prepared for this encounter, we can see that we are being led away from conflict, towards reconciliation, to inclusion and to hope.

And so, as Jesus waits by the well in the heat of the day, a woman approaches. We can only imagine what it must have been like for her, in a culture where a woman could be divorced 'for any and every reason' (Matthew 19:3, NIV). We often think of her as one utterly disgraced in her community, having to visit the well at such a time. That may well be so, but we must remember that at this time divorces were easy for a man to come by and early death not uncommon. Whatever her circumstances, she must have known more than her share of tragedy and disappointment. She may have known deep shame and disgrace. She may well have been a rejected member of a rejected community.

And yet she, like everyone else, gets thirsty and needs water to drink and water to wash with. She is as human as everyone else. So often, we do not see people like this. So often, we make quick judgements, build fences, wonder about people's worthiness and, in our own pride and insecurity, seek to feel superior, chosen, righteous in some way. Not so Jesus.

His question, in the NIV translation, bursts through all our categories and barriers in its gentleness, its humanity. It is a question that changes everything for this woman, and for her community.

'Will you give me a drink?'

Goodness and seeing truly

Jesus humbly admits his own thirst, his own need. If we have heard the parable of the sheep and the goats (Matthew 25:31–46), this question may have a deep resonance for us, for there Jesus says that whoever gives a thirsty person water, gives it to him. This story in John gives us a way of thinking about the needs before us. How would we respond – how do we respond – if a stranger asks us for a drink?

This woman is startled. Jesus speaks, not to rebuke her, but to make himself vulnerable before her, and to call out her goodness. For this is what the question does: it recognises her goodness. It recognises and awakens this truth about her – that she is someone kind enough to give a stranger a drink. It greets her as one made in the image of God, a God-bearer in the world. That image can be buried beneath layers of hiding, of shame; buried under words of condemnation that cling; it can be twisted by hatred and fear and darkness – but it is always there, and Jesus sees it. She thought that he, too, would despise her and reject her. She was wrong. How destructive it can be for us to be judged and condemned. Contrary to what those who judge may intend, it withers the shoots of goodness. It makes it harder for us to be anything other than the names we are called.

How good it is that Jesus commands us not to judge! How good that he gives to outcasts the gift of his presence, his full attention.

This woman was on the other side of several divides. If a Jewish man shared a drinking vessel with a Samaritan woman, he would be ritually unclean, contaminated, unable to worship until cleansed. For a Jewish man to speak to a woman at all was a very serious breach. The woman knows this and responds with disbelief, but the surprise does its work. It opens up the encounter for a deeper conversation where both people are able to speak truly.

Jesus points out that she does not know who is speaking to her. Of course not! Neither does she know the gift of God. Jesus is revealing both of these things gently. Perhaps she will come to see that Jesus is the gift, and he has living water. We are going deeper now. Living, life-giving, flowing water in a hot land, to a parched and weary soul, is life itself. It is a daily necessity and a joy. We know that in John, there is often an association between water and Spirit. Jesus' previous encounter with Nicodemus (in chapter 3) reveals that. The Spirit can be to us as water on a parched land, softening, enlivening, refreshing and freeing the seeds locked in dry husks, so they grow and flourish and flower.

This water that Jesus gives can become a spring in us, as indeed the Spirit in us is a spring, bubbling and welling up to life. It is life that Jesus is offering.

Zoe: life

Now, this life: the Greek word *zoe* expresses ideas we have not always captured well in English. It is more about a quality of life than a destination: a life that is abundant and pure and overflowing and goes on and on, much as the water in a bubbling spring does. It is a life, the kingdom life, that Jesus spoke of as being close at hand, now, here, with you, within you… and a life that does not end, too. It is a means of travel, as well as a destination. And the Samaritan woman wants it. I do not think she fully grasps what he means. She is still in the world of practical hard work of drawing water from the well, but I do believe there is something in what Jesus says, and perhaps in the way he says it, that opens up the possibility of more. Whatever it is, it speaks to a deep longing; it draws her with the possibility of a different sort of life.

Known and loved

Then Jesus interrupts her talk of wells, and we go down deeper still. He speaks into the pain of her situation and he touches a wounded place: her history of broken relationships. He asks her to fetch her husband. This water he promises will wash wounds, will cleanse and heal the broken places, the shameful things. He gets to the heart of her life, her isolation, her pain. Water always flows down to the lowest place; it needs to, here, to do its work of healing and restoring. We do not know what has gone wrong for her – with this lack of husband, or her many husbands – but we are not invited to weigh blame. Instead, notice how Jesus brackets his words about her husbands, with two commendations for her own truth-speaking – 'You have spoken true...' He begins and ends his remarks with an affirmation of her for her honesty. It is a very thin basis for commendation, but it is there, and Jesus takes it.

Reading this loving and generous response reminds us of good advice given to parents, partners and friends: to notice and affirm good, to praise far more than to point out shortcomings. This woman was probably well aware of the names she was called, the condemnation with which others regarded her. Did this help her to change direction? I think it made it harder. I think we can easily become the things we are called and end up calling ourselves. The names spoken over us can bind us. They can act like a curse on us. So she did not need Jesus to call her a sinner; she needed Jesus to call her honest. This woman did not respond to Jesus' statement about her numerous husbands with shame; she did not seem to feel rebuked. Later, when she runs back to the town, she tells people about the man who told her everything she ever did, echoing the calling of Nathaniel (John 1:43–50). Her response is closer to wonder.

Perhaps what affected this woman most was that even when the truth of her story was known, she was not rejected. I think we all know the longing to be fully known and yet fully loved and accepted. I believe it is almost impossible for us to face the shadows and darkness within our own heart, to bring things out into the light to be dealt with, unless we know that we will be accepted if we do. To start with judgement, or the fear of judgement, leads to hiding, as it did in the garden of Eden (Genesis 3). And yet, even there, God came looking, seeking Adam and Eve. He calls them out of their hiding.

We need to feel safe enough, loved enough, to deal with the things that need dealing with. We long to be both loved and known, but we can be deeply afraid that, if we take off our masks, we will be rejected. In order to stop hiding from God in the bushes, in order to walk with God in the cool of the evening, we need to know something of what God is like.

God is love

Do we, can we, believe that God is love? Do we trust that love is the deepest truth there is?

It can be hard to believe these things, especially if we too have known our share of tragedy and disappointment, of hostility and judgement as this woman had. Perhaps we can remember John's words at the beginning of the gospel, what he hoped to show us: 'No one has ever seen God. It is God the only Son, who is close to the Father's heart, who has made him known' (1:18). If Jesus is making God known, then we see here something of the Father's heart. We see it is open. It may be possible to find courage to open up our own heart's defences, to receive, to be healed and forgiven and restored, and so take a few tentative steps in this dance of love, of new life.

If we can know we are loved and accepted, perhaps we can engage in the hard work of loving each other in the same way – even loving our enemies and returning good for evil. If we think God is harsh and judgemental, we tend to behave that way ourselves. Jesus reminds us (Matthew 5:38–48; 7:1–5) to be imitators of God in how we behave – and how we behave can indeed reveal what we think God is like. God sends the sun and the rain to all because of his nature, not because of our worth. He forgives us for the same reason. So we seek to treat others as we know God treats us; we seek to treat each other with humility and respect, regarding each other as a holy mystery, known to God and loved by God. Perhaps we may even come to see that the thirsty person who asks us for a drink could be Christ himself (Matthew 25:31–46).

Mountains and temples

The woman at the well asks a question, a question about worship. It could be she is deliberately changing the subject, moving away from the talk of husbands. Indeed, it is often thought so. I think not – or not entirely. I think that this woman, who makes reference so determinedly to Jacob as her father, has been thinking about worship and what it means. I think she has a genuine thirst for God. Now, at last, she has someone before her who can talk to her about the things of God. And Jesus does so.

Jesus talks about the mountain and the temple, but he says that a new age is breaking through, and is now here, when such distinctions will no longer matter; that God is Spirit; and that God seeks worshippers who are kindred, who will worship in Spirit and in truth. The boundaries are smashed between temple and mountain; it is spirit and truth that matter. How much better to think in terms of authentic, life-giving worship, which helps you connect more deeply with God, with yourself, with people around you – worship which supports you in your quest to love the Lord your God, heart, soul and mind, and love your neighbour as yourself. Such worship will not exclude or condemn another. It will not get hung up on superficial differences in style. It will be open, curious and responsive to the flow of the Spirit. These are the things that Jesus begins to explain to the woman, who in her turn takes the conversation on.

> The woman said to him, 'I know that Messiah is coming' (who is called Christ). 'When he comes, he will proclaim all things to us.' Jesus said to her, 'I am he, the one who is speaking to you.'
> JOHN 4:25-26

We have reached the 'I am' moment: the Greek in which John records Jesus' reply is *ego eimi*, 'I am', the same as the other 'I am' statements. She, a Samaritan, declares that she too is waiting for the Messiah, and Jesus in turn declares that he is the one she waits for. Barriers continue to be broken down. It is to this woman, in this place, that Jesus declares his identity. This is a truly astonishing moment.

At that moment, the disciples return and the conversation stops at this high peak. The woman leaves her water jug behind and runs back to the town. We do not know how much meaning John gives the abandoned water jug. Perhaps it signifies her leaving behind her old life, with its old sources of water. We do not know, but we do know her life changes. She becomes an evangelist to the Samaritans, bringing them to Jesus as Philip brought Nathaniel. She is someone her neighbours listen to. We see the new life bubbling up in her already. We do not know what happens about her domestic arrangements, her husbands or lack of them; that detail is not recorded for us. We do, however, see what this new life, bubbling over, means and what it looks like. We see that it is in Samaria that Jesus acknowledges the title of Messiah, and that it is the Samaritans who call him 'Saviour of the world' – a title for the Roman Emperor. They saw Jesus as something bigger than even Judea and Samaria, as big as they could imagine. Typically, it was those outside the categories of chosen people who saw that this Messiah was for the whole world.

This encounter, which started with a request for water, has become the source, the spring, of transformation that changed a whole community. Jesus gives value to a person, and to a whole people, who were despised. Here, in the heat of the day, they were offered fresh, life-giving water. And they drank from this new well.

Reflection and response

Study

John 4:1–6

- How do you respond to:
  - the background details of the story – do they help?
  - the Pharisees and the possibility of conflict with John?
  - the physical setting, at Jacob's well?
  - the details about Joseph? (See Joshua 24:32 – many think Sychar and Shechem are the same place.)
- Why do you think Jesus travelled this way? Have you taken unconventional routes at any time? Why or why not?

John 4:7–15

- Have you ever been asked for a drink by a stranger? What happened? Have you ever needed someone to give you a drink? What was that like?
- Are there people you would be reluctant to talk to and drink with? If so, why? Your reasons may be valid.
- What do you understand by 'the gift of God', and 'living water'?
- What differences do you notice between the two sorts of water – the water from the well and the water Jesus is offering?
- When the woman says 'our ancestor Jacob', who do you think she meant by 'our'? What does her question tell you about her?

John 4:16–26

- Why do you think Jesus told her to go and get her husband?
- Some commentators suggest the husbands represent the Assyrian tribes and their gods. What do you think of the possibility of a literal and a figurative reading? (See 2 Kings 17:24.)
- Do you worship? Where and how? Have there been times in your life when you have worshipped differently?
- What does this passage suggest about differences in styles of worship?
- What does worshipping in Spirit and in truth mean to you?
- What do you understand by 'God is Spirit'?
- Have you had experiences of worship which have made a difference to you?

John 4:27–42

- Why might the woman have left when the disciples returned?
- Do you attach any significance to the woman leaving behind her water jug?
- This is the second example of someone bringing others to Jesus in this gospel, the first being Philip (1:43–51). Do you see any similarities or differences?
- Have you had experience of sharing your faith?
- How did you come to faith, or how are you coming to faith? What helps you believe?
- What significance do you attach to the fact that the first people to call Jesus 'Saviour of the world' were Samaritans?

Further study

- Matthew 25:31–46. How does the woman at the well help you understand this parable?
- John 3:1–21. In what ways is Nicodemus' encounter like that with the woman at the well, and in what ways different? What can we learn from the common threads, and the differences of approach?
- Luke 10:25–37 – the parable of the good Samaritan. Reflect on what it means to love your neighbour.

Passages with a water theme

- Exodus 17:1–7
- Ezekiel 47:1–12
- Psalm 42 (especially vv. 1–4, 7)
- Psalm 63 (especially v. 1)
- John 7:37–39
- Revelation 22:1–3

Prayer and meditation

Thanksgiving for water

For one day, give thanks every time you use water in any way. If you make purchases, wear clean clothes or eat food out, give thanks for the water involved in those processes. You might wish to meditate on baptism or living water while in the shower or bath.

In Gloucester Cathedral cloisters, there are stained glass windows illustrating water-based stories above the place where the monks washed. You might like to find a picture of these and place it by your sink or kitchen tap. You could use this prayer every time you use it:

> Dear God, thank you for the gift of life-giving water. Thank you that by it we can be clean and quench our thirst. Help us remember how you make us clean and give us living water. Help us to help those who have no water. Amen

On thirst and water

Pour out a jug of water and set it before you, together with a glass. Ask yourself what you thirst for. Allow honest answers to emerge and note them. Where does your life feel dry and unproductive? What would help?

Reflect on some verses from the water passages in 'Further study' above.

Pour yourself water, and drink as much as you like, deliberately savouring it.

Appreciate what it means to have your thirst quenched. Think again of Jesus' promise of living water welling up inside you. Accept that promise for yourself. What might it mean for you to quench your thirst with Jesus?

When you have finished, find a place outside to pour out any remaining water, where it will do good. As you pour, watch the water, where it flows, what it does. Think of living water flowing to dry places in your life and community. Pray for them, that they may receive the water of life.

Prayer for everyday activity
The woman met Jesus through an everyday activity. Is there a chore or task you do regularly, perhaps without much joy? Why not turn it into an opportunity for prayer? You might like to write a one-line prayer you can remember, or to use it as an opportunity to become aware of God with you. Offer it to God as an act of service – like giving a drink to Jesus at the well.

Creative response

Pick a phrase that strikes you from this Bible passage – mine is 'the well is deep'. Explore what it conjures up in you, writing poetry or prose, a story or whatever other form suits you.

You could explore the theme of living water in another media – flowing paints or watercolour might be appropriate. Spend time quietly, dwelling on the story, and then work with your brush.

This story seems ideally suited to being interpreted visually.

Life and service

Lay down your measuring sticks

We can all fall into the trap of comparing, measuring. Sometimes, we can be prone to envy, judgement or rivalry. Notice what Jesus does when the Pharisees compare (4:1) – he removes himself from the situation.

Ask God to help you see as God sees this day – as beloved children of the same heavenly Father. If you notice yourself comparing yourself to another – maybe their age, weight, education level, car or clothing – stop. Bless them instead. Thank God for them. Pray that they may have love, hope, health and security in their lives.

Read Philippians 2:3.

I will give you a new name

Read Revelation 2:17. We may have been bullied, shamed, called names – by people at school, a parent, a boss or even the church. If that has been your experience, if you find those old names keep resurfacing, you could try the following:

Write down those names that have hurt you on scraps of paper and then scrub them out and write a name from the promises of God. You could write: beloved, God's workmanship, chosen, precious, honoured, redeemed, forgiven, set free, etc. If you are doing this as a group activity, perhaps you could take turns to speak out good things to each other.

Maybe God has a new name for you. You could ask, in prayer, for a new name, and write down what comes to mind. Then, if something comes, take some time to find out the meaning of the name and reflect on why it may have come to you.

Write your new or chosen name on a stone – a white one if you can find one – and treasure it.

'I was thirsty and you gave me a drink'

In our story, Jesus asks for a drink. In the parable of the sheep and the goats, Jesus identifies with the thirsty.

Many lack drinking water and sanitation, including people in our own cities without secure housing. Clean, safe water is good news for those without, and the cost of providing it is modest.

Find out about places and people who lack water, and pray for them.

Pray, too, for charities who work to provide water and sanitation, e.g. Tearfund, Toilet Twinning, homeless charities in your area.

You could raise or give money. If you buy drinks out, perhaps you could fast from one or two a week, and give the money to a charity instead.

You could carry extra bottles of water to give to the homeless or buy tea or coffee for those you encounter and drink with them. I have gift vouchers for coffee shops in my bag to pass on.

You could donate drinks to a food bank.

Reflect on your experience of doing any of the above. Have you encountered a thirsty Jesus? Can you see this as worship and Christian service?

Barriers and divisions

Maybe there are people, or groups of people, you automatically distrust. Sometimes this is unthinking, but sometimes it is sound instinct. Boundaries are very necessary to keep ourselves and others from harm. So we seek God's wisdom, and pray to see clearly and lovingly. Where you can, stretch out a hand to someone outside your normal circle. We can bless people in prayer and seek to become warm-hearted towards them.

Could this be the Messiah?
Following on from the study questions, you might like to consider ways to share your faith experience with others. The book *Sowing, Reaping, Keeping* by Laurence Singlehurst[2] is really helpful for this.

Beginnings can be small; spend time developing deeper relationships with people – because you want to learn to love and care for them. Share from your own life's story. Say a little and wait for questions. Don't worry if they don't come. Be gentle. Use language people will understand.

Worship
Read through the story in John 4 slowly, focusing on the character of Jesus. Then move to an attitude of thanks and praise. You might like to choose some music to help you in your worship, to express what this story means for you, and how you are welcomed and accepted into the kingdom.

Take one day to try to incorporate worship in various ways into your life. You could write out some prayers of worship. You could listen to music or allow music to fill your mind. You could seek to see service to others as an act of worship. Make a conscious effort to turn to God, who is Spirit, and the worship of God, during the day. You could use an alarm to remind you every hour, or use a prayer or worship app.

You could try an unfamiliar style of worship or worship music, entering into it in Spirit and truth.

Further reading

Brian McLaren, *A Generous Orthodoxy* (Zondervan, 2004)
Marilynne Robinson, *Lila* (Farrar, Straus and Giroux, 2014) – a novel
Laurence Singlehurst, *Sowing, Reaping, Keeping* (InterVarsity Press, 2006)
Desmond Tutu, *Made for Goodness* (Harper, 2010)
Nadia Bolz Weber, *Accidental Saints* (Canterbury Press, 2015)

3

I am the bread of life

After this Jesus went away to the other side of the Sea of Galilee, which is the Sea of Tiberias. And a large crowd was following him, because they saw the signs that he was doing on the sick. Jesus went up on the mountain, and there he sat down with his disciples. Now the Passover, the feast of the Jews, was at hand. Lifting up his eyes, then, and seeing that a large crowd was coming towards him, Jesus said to Philip, 'Where are we to buy bread, so that these people may eat?' He said this to test him, for he himself knew what he would do. Philip answered him, 'Two hundred denarii would not buy enough bread for each of them to get a little.' One of his disciples, Andrew, Simon Peter's brother, said to him, 'There is a boy here who has five barley loaves and two fish, but what are they for so many?' Jesus said, 'Make the people sit down.' Now there was much grass in the place. So the men sat down, about five thousand in number. Jesus then took the loaves, and when he had given thanks, he distributed them to those who were seated. So also the fish, as much as they wanted. And when they had eaten their fill, he told his disciples, 'Gather up the leftover fragments, that nothing may be lost.' So they gathered them up and filled twelve baskets with fragments from the five barley loaves left by those who had eaten. When the people saw the sign that he had done, they said, 'This is indeed the Prophet who is to come into the world!'

Perceiving then that they were about to come and take him by force to make him king, Jesus withdrew again to the mountain by himself...

When they found him on the other side of the sea, they said to him, 'Rabbi, when did you come here?' Jesus answered them, 'Truly, truly, I say to you, you are seeking me, not because you saw signs, but because you ate your fill of the loaves. Do not labour for the food that perishes, but for the food that endures to eternal life, which the Son of Man will give to you. For on him God the Father has set his seal.' Then they said to him, 'What must we do, to be doing the works of God?' Jesus answered them, 'This is the work of God, that you believe in him whom he has sent.' So they said to him, 'Then what sign do you do, that we may see and believe you? What work do you perform? Our fathers ate the manna in the wilderness; as it is written, "He gave them bread from heaven to eat."' Jesus then said to them, 'Truly, truly, I say to you, it was not Moses who gave you the bread from heaven, but my Father gives you the true bread from heaven. For the bread of God is he who comes down from heaven and gives life to the world.' They said to him, 'Sir, give us this bread always.'

Jesus said to them, 'I am the bread of life; whoever comes to me shall not hunger, and whoever believes in me shall never thirst.

JOHN 6:1–15, 25–35 (ESV)

Bread and life

Jesus fed a hungry crowd. They had followed him to a remote place by the lake, where there was nowhere for them to get food. There, he gave them bread to sustain them, and later he said he himself was bread – bread that came down from heaven, the bread of life for the world. Not surprisingly, they were mystified.

For millennia, bread has been the most basic food, the stuff of life. Many a hungry belly has yearned for bread. It is food for all, but especially for the poorest. It is simple – not food to tempt a jaded gourmet or for an elaborate banquet – and yet the smell of good bread is warming, joyful, one of the delights of life. Jesus says he comes to us in the ordinary, the daily, in the good and satisfying.

Bread also reminds us of something about ourselves that we can easily forget – that we are dependent on the earth and each other for food. Many of us have lost a daily connection with the earth. We can be deluded that we are somehow above the elements that make us. It takes humility to remember we are bound to the earth, to the rain and the sun, that we are part of the dust. The second account of creation reminds us that we are *adamah* (meaning earth or ground, Genesis 2:7) and part of all things, formed from earth. As bread is blessed in a Communion service, we remember and give thanks for the fruit of the earth and the work of human hands. So, in bread, we have a reminder that we are dependent on God's provision through the whole of creation – earth, rain, light, wind. We remember too that we are part of a community, connected with others on whom we depend. We remember that we are part of all things, and God has blessed all things and called them good. In this one simple thing, bread, we see God's goodness.

Not by bread alone

At the very beginning of his ministry, Jesus spent time in the wilderness where he fasted, prayed and was tempted. One of the temptations the hungry Jesus faced was turning stones into bread. Jesus answered, 'It is written, "One does not live by bread alone, but by every word that comes from the mouth of God"' (Matthew 4:1–4). The dangers of receiving 'bread alone' seem to unfold through the rest of the story, but as Jesus answers the temptation we are reminded of a deep thread in Hebrew thought – that the wisdom, the mind of God, the Word, nourishes and sustains us like food. Ezekiel had a scroll to eat (Ezekiel 2:8–3:3), and the psalmists, too, describe God's words as sweet as honey (e.g. Psalm 19:10; 119:103). God feeds us like bread. This way of seeing helps us remember that our inbuilt need for God is a deep hunger.

In Jesus, tempted in the wilderness, we see a paradox. Jesus, this Word made flesh, feels hunger like us, needs bread like us. Now, astonishingly, after this feeding of hungry people, he says he is bread, and that he will be broken for us. This Word made flesh has become bread for us. Let us return to the story to see what this might mean.

Firstly, we notice who was fed: everyone, all that multitude. Here, we see the extravagant generosity of Jesus, and the extent of human need. Bread was given to all the hungry people who were in the crowd: there is no payment, no worthiness criteria, no belief criteria in this feeding; simply, if you come, you will be fed.

All who need it receive bread.

> From his fullness we have all received, grace upon grace.
> JOHN 1:16

It is freely given to those who need it: that is the nature of grace. Jesus makes God known, and God is generous, giving life to all.

We see too that this bread is shared in a wild place - even there, Jesus feeds us. When it seems that there is nothing to eat, when we are in a barren place, away from markets and empires and temples, even there Jesus feeds us. For we all grow hungry.

We must all eat. To eat the bread of life may be more practice than theology. We must simply take and eat. Maybe it is in the taking and eating that we come to understand. One way to take and eat is in the sharing of Communion, the centre of many Christian gatherings. As we trust in the sustaining power of God, we can recognise Jesus there.

There is a story at the end of Luke's gospel (24:13–35). Two of Jesus' disciples, Cleopas and possibly his wife Mary, walked away from Jerusalem to Emmaus after the death of Jesus. A strange figure joins them, asks them their sorrow and explains to them why the

Messiah had to die. They do not know who it is, but when they sit down and eat with him, when he gives thanks for the bread and breaks it before them, then they know it is Jesus. Sometimes it is in moments of hospitality, community and generosity, in moments of blessing and breaking and sharing bread, that we come to see what is beyond the power of our minds to know. Maybe we need to taste, to eat, to satisfy our hunger. We come hungry to the presence of Jesus, but we may not know it is Jesus we hunger for. He always gives us bread and not stones (Matthew 7:9–11). We are sustained, nourished, by an encounter with Jesus, by this act of eating, even as we do not understand. There is a deep humility in entering into the flow of love, grace and forgiveness from God, knowing it is beyond our mind's grasp. By eating this bread, we receive grace beyond our understanding.

Enough, and thanks

And, so, the people all ate. There was enough. One of the many things this miraculous sign does is take our natural fear of 'not enough' – and offer God's 'enough' instead. We find it hard to be generous when there are only a few small loaves and fish, and so many hungry people. With Jesus, we see a picture of what it means to shift our perspective, to reframe our notions.

Firstly, the boy must have handed his food to Jesus or to Andrew. That was a big step. It is hard to let go of the little we believe we have and put it into the hands of Jesus. The very idea of putting things into the hands of Jesus can sound a little quaint, but perhaps, again, it is a thing best practised, tried.

What if we began seeing what we had – not in terms of what it was not, but in terms of what it was? Of seeing things not as our resource, but as a kingdom resource? This is food, these people need food, that's what we'll do – give. Of course, the rational counting and measuring parts of our minds are not satisfied with that, and we are grateful for the stock control systems and emergency relief managers who count well enough to make sure all can be fed, but perhaps this is a different kind of lesson: one that turns our minds from what we see to the God of abundance. Perhaps even this small act of generosity is magnified, amplified by a God who loves and longs to be generous. What if each small act in the direction of goodness has consequences beyond our imagining?

What if each small act of love, of giving, of sharing, receives a blessing, a thanksgiving from Jesus? Imagine what the world would be like if we believed that, and then acted accordingly.

And so, we see what Jesus does with the little he has been given by a child: he takes it in his hands, gives thanks and then gives it away. There is no description of how so many are fed. All we see and know is that Jesus takes, gives thanks and gives away. He gives thanks for the little he holds in his hands *before* it is enough. This is another practice we can engage with: thanksgiving. It is a powerful way of shifting us from a perspective of scarcity and anxiety to one of gratitude, of noticing the good and the blessing and the small loaves among so many hungry people. The Greek word for thanksgiving is *eucharisteo* – from which we get one of our words for the bread and wine we share together, the Eucharist. Within it are nestled other meanings – *charis*, grace; *chara*, joy. Thanks, grace and joy are caught up with each other. To live a life in gratitude, to look for reasons to give thanks, is to see the grace we are receiving each moment and to respond with a joy that is deep, that gives a bedrock even in sorrow. Gratitude changes things – especially us.

Nothing is wasted

Jesus models many things here for his followers: compassion for the hungry, a desire to help, seeing much in little and giving thanks. After all have eaten, Jesus tells the disciples to gather all the broken fragments up, and there are twelve basketfuls. Nothing is wasted.

Twelve, of course, is a powerful number for this nation: the number of the tribes, representing the whole people. This passage calls to mind references to gathering what has been lost and scattered among the nations (see Jeremiah 31:10). It helps us remember that nothing is wasted in God's economy. Jesus comes to restore all things and make all things new (Revelation 21:5); the work of God is about transforming what seems beyond mending. All our mistakes, disasters and tragedies, all that is lost, spoilt and broken in ourselves and our lives – all can be gathered up and redeemed. Jesus seems to gloss his meaning later: 'And this is the will of him who sent me, that I should lose nothing of all that he has given me, but raise it up on the last day' (John 6:39). Nothing will be lost, either in the apparently small matter of wasted food, or in the great 'all' of 'all that he has given me'. It matters. All of it.

As we seek to find ways of living out these 'I am' sayings, perhaps we too can be a people who gather up the broken pieces, so that nothing and no one is wasted and lost. It humbles us; it involves us stooping and searching for each broken thing. By gathering the broken, we are following Jesus' instruction *and* example. The kingdom is the very opposite of a throwaway society.

Prophet and king?

So the disciples tidy up after the picnic, and perhaps we imagine childhood summers, with gentle sunshine and soft grass. This al fresco eating was like that, but also very different. Some who were there did not see it as a picnic – more as a call to arms. The crowds, having eaten the bread, called Jesus the 'prophet who is to come into the world' (6:14), and they tried to make him king by force. The irony seemed to escape them, as it escapes us so often, when we confidently co-opt God into our own agenda. A king you can force is no king, more a projection of your own desires. It is hard to be humble enough to see this. But Jesus sees it and, as ever, steps to the side (6:15).

He is not the king the crowds seek, even though he is King. The crowds see this event drawing on the old stories of liberation and salvation and Moses in the wilderness. They see it as a Passover feast, even as they are mistaken about what that means. No one here is imagining Jesus could be the lamb slain. They seem to imagine him leading the overthrow of the Romans, as Moses liberated them from the Egyptians. And yet John records that it is nearly Passover. There is a connection. This is a liberation feast. It is also manna, food for the journey to sustain the freed slaves in the wilderness. Jesus, the bread from heaven, is both of these things: food at a table where we gather together, food in our pockets as we walk into freedom and as we walk home (see Exodus 12 and 16).

Walking on water

John's writing on the bread of life falls into two parts. There is the account of the sign, at which we have been looking (6:1–15), and also the rather tense discussion which follows (6:22–71). But there is a strange interlude in the story, between the sign and the discussion, where we find the disciples rowing against a sudden and strong wind in the dark, without Jesus. To row three or four miles in such conditions would be both terrifying and exhausting. The muscles burn and tear, and the dark, stormy waters fill their minds with the thought of sinking, of drowning. Then, far from shore, they see someone come towards them over the water, and a different kind of fear overtakes them. It is at this moment that Jesus speaks. He says, in the Greek, *ego eimi* (6:20), the same phrase as the other 'I am' sayings. Then: 'Do not be afraid.' In the midst of darkness and danger, Jesus' presence was with them. Perhaps this strange story contains another echo of the exodus – where a mysterious presence goes with the people and shows them the way. A pillar of fire and of cloud. Perhaps this was how Jesus was to them, too: a saving and guiding presence.

A sign of the kingdom

Then, the next day, the crowds find him again, and the discussions begin. We are getting close now to the moment when Jesus says, 'I am the bread of life.' But we are not there quite yet. Before, Jesus says they come to him not because they understand what has happened, but because their hunger was filled. The meaning of the sign seems to escape them. Then, he continues: 'Do not work for the food that perishes, but for the food that endures to eternal life' (6:27), drawing on a passage in Isaiah 55. Here, we brush against another layer of meaning, and another way that we are fed by God.

> Come, everyone who thirsts,
> come to the waters;
> and he who has no money,
> come, buy and eat!
> Come, buy wine and milk
> without money and without price.
> Why do you spend your money for that which is not bread,
> and your labour for that which does not satisfy?
> Listen diligently to me, and eat what is good,
> and delight yourselves in rich food.
> Incline your ear, and come to me;
> hear, that your soul may live;
> and I will make with you an everlasting covenant,
> my steadfast, sure love for David.
>
> ISAIAH 55:1–3 (ESV)

This whole beautiful passage on the faithfulness of God reminds us that God's ways are higher than ours, above ours: generous, forgiving, reconciling, nourishing. This radical passage speaks of grace and undermines our dependence on a system where money is everything. Maybe in God's kingdom, there will be enough. God is calling to us like someone running a market stall, offering the finest produce for free.

Come.

God's words are needed now, as we are trapped in cycles of 'getting and spending'[3] which consume us. We labour for many things which do not satisfy us. We also apply these same principles to our spiritual lives – our labour for God, which may be good works or good systems of belief or good attendance, are not the things which satisfy, nor are they needed by God. The wine and milk that God freely offers us – they delight us, restore us.

Certainly, here is rich soul food that delights and brings life. It is such a powerful frame for viewing Jesus as the bread of life. He is reminding us that what God offers is an everlasting love that cannot be shaken.

We are so easily distracted from it, so easily overwhelmed by other voices, by other demands, but it is there, calling, like the market stallholder who draws customers day after day. And later on in the Isaiah passage, we read of how creation itself will echo the delight spoken of: the snows will nourish and water the earth; plants will grow again; sweetness, goodness and delight will rise up in fragrance and growth. Nature's reciprocal giving and growing and interdependence reveal something of the mind and nature of God. Hard times will pass. There is hope. This flourishing is also echoed in Jesus' words, 'For the bread of God is that which comes down from heaven and gives life to the world' (6:33), where the Greek word translated as 'world' is *cosmos*.

The bread may be without price, but Jesus does mention work. The 'work' here is believing in the one God has sent. Perhaps Jesus is making a light-hearted contrast, as he speaks to people used to backbreaking labour to earn bread and used to exacting legal observance to keep their religious standing. Just trust. Just accept. That's all the work you need.

'Heaven in ordinary'

George Herbert's sonnet 'Prayer'[4] is a list of extraordinary phrases exploring what prayer means. One of them is this – 'heaven in ordinary'. It is a way we can think about Jesus as the bread, from heaven, which is also the bread of life.

> For the bread of God is that which comes down from heaven and gives life to the world.
>
> JOHN 6:33

Much of what Jesus says in this discussion (6:30–51) is misunderstood – incomprehensible, even, to his first hearers – but we have begun to open up his meaning by looking at the sign, the feeding of the 5,000. There is always more.

The bread is that which 'gives life to the world'. And all 'that' is embodied in something as ordinary as bread, as ordinary as a carpenter's son from Nazareth. Can we, in our ordinary lives, find this deep nourishment from God? Can we be sustained and united with Jesus in these small daily things?

What is food for your soul? Can you eat of it this very day?

John's gospel does not talk about the bread and the wine at the final meal Jesus shares with his friends: here is where we find Jesus speaking about his body and his blood, as he looks ahead to when he is broken for us on the cross. We can look at this offering of food in a wilderness, this extravagant grace and generosity and thanksgiving, and see in it a model for how Jesus gave himself for us all. But his hearers were bewildered, not knowing what is to come.

Some stay with him, though. They stay not because they understand this teaching but, as Peter says, because they know who Jesus is, know that his words give life and know too there is nowhere else for them to go (6:68–69).

Even if we do not fully understand, maybe we can echo Peter's words, respond to this invitation and let Jesus nourish us and sustain us. Maybe we can develop practices of giving thanks, of breaking and sharing bread in our daily lives that connect us more deeply with each other and with Jesus. Maybe we can sit in his presence and take delight in good food, so that our souls rejoice.

See how ordinary it all is, how God comes to us as bread. We can find in our daily lives, in our lived experience, a deep communion. There have been fresh expressions of church, for example the Bread Church set up by Barbara Glasson[5] in the UK, where communities have been brought together through the practice of making bread, where the making and eating of bread has become the basis for a common life. Our toddler group was warmed by the smell of toast, a smell of home. There are many ways that bread can be part of our community and worship, the provision of bread part of our love and service to all. We can feed, as we are fed.

And there, we can remember that this is a gospel of transformation: taking what we are, all our broken pieces, all the smallness we feel in ourselves, and making us new – making us enough in Christ. This is bread for the journey, bread in the hard and barren places where we desperately need it. And, so, nourished on our way, maybe we too can enter into this great 'I am', and be part of bringing bread to a hungry world.

Reflection and response

Study

John 6:1–15, 30–33

- John calls these events 'signs'. What does that suggest to you? What do we learn about the kingdom from this one?
- Consider the way Jesus involves his disciples in this event. What can we learn about our role in the kingdom?

John 6:25–59

- It seems that Jesus wanted these people to go deeper than thinking of their physical hunger. What do you understand verse 28 to mean? How might that work out in practice?
- Trace the idea of bread from heaven through this passage. How does it nourish? How does it sustain?
- Look at the ways Jesus talks about his relationship with the Father in this passage, and then his relationship with us. What can we learn about that deep interconnectedness?
- John does not give us an account of the bread and wine at the last supper. Might this discourse give us an insight into it nonetheless?

Further study

- Compare this passage with the story of the exodus. In what ways is it similar, and different? See Exodus 12:43–50; 14—16. You might also like to read the story of the road to Emmaus in Luke 24:13–35.
- How do you respond to the idea of eating the word? See Ezekiel 2:8—3:3, Psalms (e.g. 19:10; 119:103) and Jesus' reply to the temptation (Matthew 4:3–4; Deuteronomy 8:3). Philo of Alexandria (25BC–AD50, *Commentaries on the Pentateuch* and *de Vita Mosis*) said the manna given to the Jewish people is another way of talking about how God sustained the people in the wilderness – with *Logos*, with wisdom.[6] Some have seen the two loaves and five fish as being like the two stone tablets and five books of the law of Moses. How do you respond to that suggestion?

- Read 1 Corinthians 11:17–33. How does this church 'communion' fall short, if it does? Continue by reading chapters 12—13.

Prayer and meditation

Enough, not enough?

Sometimes we can look at the little we have at our disposal and the greatness of the needs we see, and be overwhelmed. Look at the exchange between Andrew and Jesus. What have you to offer? Where do you feel a lack? Meditate on this scene, bringing objects that represent what you have and where you feel a lack, and lay them before you. Use words and paper if more practical. Ask Jesus to bless them and give thanks for them.

Make a practice of always doing the little you can, and asking Jesus to bless and multiply it. What do you notice as you do so?

One-word prayer prompts

Adopt the model of one word, or short phrase, to focus your prayer as you go about your day. You could use: Love, Grace, Thanks, Enough, Joy, Basket, Bread, Give… or something else from the passage.

Thanksgiving

Use this passage to refresh your gratitude for food. Pause to give thanks for everything you eat and drink today. If you routinely do so, try to ensure it is not just habit, but meaningful.

Lord Jesus, who broke bread beside the lake and all were fed,
thank you for feeding us.
Lord Jesus, who asked his disciples to pass food to the crowds,
may we do the same.
Lord Jesus, who saw to it that all the spare food was gathered,
may we let no good thing go to waste.
Lord Jesus, who gave thanks,
we thank you now.[7]

You could use a symbol and reminder for prayer, like a candle or a small object on your table, especially if out-loud prayer is difficult in your situation.

Creative response

Bread-making

If making bread is impractical, buy some nice bread, and seeds or cooked grain, and spend longer meditating on the verses. If you are making bread, use a recipe of your choice.

Preparing and mixing. As you gather and mix your ingredients, hold in your mind Jesus' words: the mustard seed (Matthew 13:31–32; 17:20), the growing seed (Mark 4:26–27), the parable of the sower (Luke 8:4–15), yeast (Luke 13:18–21), grains falling to the ground (John 12:24).

Kneading and rising. As you knead and then leave the dough to rise, continue to dwell on those words. Think how things grow and develop in their own time, how grain takes time to reach fruitfulness. Consider how God chooses to involve us in his work, like the kneading, but the growth is his. Consider patience.

Knocking back. Read Exodus 16:1–17. What must it have been like to receive manna, God's provision, in the desert? Enough for each day, even in barren places.

Second rising. Read John 6, the feeding of the 5,000. Dwell on God's abundant provision.

Baking. As the smell of bread fills your home, what does it mean for you to feed on Jesus daily? How is Jesus your bread of life?

Breaking and eating. Perhaps you can share your bread. How can Jesus be the bread of life in your community? Are there practical ways you and your church can show love and care?

Pray a prayer of thankfulness over your bread and ask God to sustain you and others through it, and through Jesus, the bread of life. End by reading Luke 24:30–32.

Life and service

Keep a gratitude journal

Every evening, look back at the day and write down five things you would like to give thanks for. You can also have a journal or an app with you at all times to record as many opportunities for gratitude as you can.

Variation: take a gratitude walk. Each day, as you walk, look for as many things to be thankful for as you can.

Support bread-makers

If there are bakers or bread-makers in your community, support them if you can. Try different types of bread. Try making and sharing bread with your neighbours.

Bread for a hungry world: social action

Feeding people was a sign of God's kingdom. How can we live that out where we are – open-handed – thankful for what we receive, ready to share? Perhaps there are food banks or homeless people near you for whom you can buy food. Perhaps you can cook and share what you have made. Perhaps you can support a charity that feeds the hungry.

All are fed

How can food be a sign of kingdom welcome in your community? Our church held a community hog roast and invited everyone who lived nearby. A band played, and people talked and laughed as they ate together.

Investigate Bread Church, part of the Fresh Expressions movement. Could you be involved in something like that?

Think about offering toast rather than biscuits at toddler groups and other gatherings. My parish church made bread with the children on Good Friday, to share in Communion with all on Easter Sunday. Messy Church and Alpha involve eating meals together. Many churches offer community lunches or teas.

Maybe there are ways you can demonstrate the open hospitality of the Father.

Let nothing be wasted
Set yourself a challenge for the week: to avoid waste, especially food waste.

Communion
Meditate on Jesus, the bread of life, as you experience Communion (or whatever it might be called in your church). Allow yourself to be fed. Does this feeding sustain you as you go out?

Consider sharing a meal, or bread and wine, together as a family or group, as you talk about Jesus as the bread of life.

Daily feeding on the words of Jesus
Choose some words from this passage that speak to you. Write them out and meditate on them as you go about your daily activity. You could make them into artworks, by hand or digitally, taking your time. Let them nourish and enrich you. Apps such as 'Pray as you go' can help to prompt you.

Fasting
If it is appropriate for you, consider the practice of fasting as an act of solidarity with the hungry. For example, you could fast for a day, miss a meal or abstain from a treat a couple of times a week. Meditate on both physical and other forms of hunger. If you save money while doing this, consider giving it to those who lack.

Further reading

Roy Godwin and Dave Roberts, *The Grace Outpouring* (David C. Cook, 2008)
John Ortberg, *If You Want to Walk on Water, You've Got to Get Out of the Boat* (Zondervan, 2001)
Ann Voskamp, *One Thousand Gifts* (Zondervan, 2011)

4

I am the light of the world

As he passed by, he saw a man blind from birth. And his disciples asked him, 'Rabbi, who sinned, this man or his parents, that he was born blind?' Jesus answered, 'It was not that this man sinned, or his parents, but that the works of God might be displayed in him. We must work the works of him who sent me while it is day; night is coming, when no one can work. As long as I am in the world, I am the light of the world.' Having said these things, he spat on the ground and made mud with the saliva. Then he anointed the man's eyes with the mud and said to him, 'Go, wash in the pool of Siloam' (which means Sent). So he went and washed and came back seeing.

The neighbours and those who had seen him before as a beggar were saying, 'Is this not the man who used to sit and beg?' Some said, 'It is he.' Others said, 'No, but he is like him.' He kept saying, 'I am the man.' So they said to him, 'Then how were your eyes opened?' He answered, 'The man called Jesus made mud and anointed my eyes and said to me, "Go to Siloam and wash." So I went and washed and received my sight.' They said to him, 'Where is he?' He said, 'I do not know.'

JOHN 9:1–12 (ESV)

The true light that gives light to everyone was coming into the world.

JOHN 1:9 (NIV)

Light shines through broken pieces

The Lady Chapel of Wells Cathedral was full of the most extraordinary coloured light. It fell in ribbons through the windows, which were not the usual collections of stories and saints. They were a vibrant kaleidoscope of shape and colour, exuberant and abstract, scattered with recognisable pieces of face and clothing. But this was nothing to the beauty of the light that poured through them, for it turned the morning light to wild splashes of colour, transforming all it touched – all that old stone and wood and metal – to vibrant life.

I asked someone about the glass, how it came to be, and he told me.

The medieval windows had been destroyed in the Monmouth Rebellion in 1685, poked out by pikes. After the soldiers left, the townspeople took action. They gathered up the broken pieces, crawling on their hands and knees in the dirt, risking cuts from the sharp edges. They saved the glass, even though the knowledge of how to repair it was lost. They packed the glass pieces into crates, which were stored away in the cathedral and forgotten. Centuries later, when the skills of window-making had been relearned, something new was attempted – the beautiful abstract patterns we see now.

All those broken pieces, all those jagged edges, all those lost pictures were put together in a new way, transformed into something glorious. Something new was made out of the discarded, useless pieces. And the light of the morning sun poured through them, making everything within shine, lit up with glorious colour.

I saw a parable in this glass, a kingdom story of the new creation. We, broken and discarded and small as we may be, can be held up to the light. All our broken edges can be joined together to make something harmonious and illuminating, colouring whatever our light falls on. Christ, in whom all things hold together, can indeed hold us together. Not that we are perfect or even good, but this light shines through us, transforming us, transforming everything.

You can see the parable another way, too. We can also be those people who stooped in the dirt and gathered the pieces, who saw them as precious and who kept them safe: like the disciples filling up baskets of broken bread in the previous chapter, like Jesus seeking out the rejected man in this. Jesus cared for people on the edges, the lost and the rejected.

The man who was born blind and, before that, the woman who was to be stoned were gathered up, edges and all, and illuminated by love and grace.

The woman and the stones

Jesus first says, 'I am the light of the world' in a very dark place (see John 8:1–12). The setting was the Feast of Tabernacles, or Booths, when the huge candlestick was lit at the temple, and the light from it was seen in Jerusalem's streets. It was a week-long celebration, but John's record (chapters 7—8) is not celebratory. It is tense, full of challenge and conflict between the religious leaders and Jesus. As is often the case with a conflict, the two parties seem to be looking at things through very different lenses – in this case, grace and law. This is a theme John introduces in his prologue (John 1:14–18). Jesus comes, full of grace and truth, and John says that in Jesus we can see clearly and truly, with our own eyes, what God is like. We see grace and truth. So if this is a lens, it is one that corrects our vision and gives us new sight. In these chapters, the contrast with the angry wielding of law practised by the religious leaders is hard to read.

They seem to be policing the celebrations while Jesus is teaching in the temple, an eager crowd listening to him. The religious leaders bring a woman before Jesus, caught in adultery, and ask Jesus if she should be stoned as the law demands. The woman, whose life hangs in the balance, doesn't seem to be of much concern. At this challenge, Jesus does something remarkable. He shows us a different way of seeing – a different way we can think about the law.

The law can be used to judge and condemn another, or it can be used to throw light on our own hearts and motives.

> Let anyone among you who is without sin be the first to throw a stone at her.
>
> JOHN 8:7

That is the use Jesus makes of it here, and, one by one, the religious leaders come to see it that way too, dropping their stones as they remember their own guilt. Once the danger is past, he speaks directly to her, restoring her dignity and personhood.

> 'Woman, where are they? Has no one condemned you?' She said, 'No one, sir.' And Jesus said, 'Neither do I condemn you. Go your way, and from now on do not sin again.'
>
> JOHN 8:10–11

It would have been easy for her to slip into a miserable life, her reputation so publicly destroyed, with no honourable means of support available to her. I think Jesus' words would have given her the courage to find another way of living, free and forgiven.

With the stones lying on the ground, Jesus says, 'I am the light of the world. Whoever follows me will never walk in darkness, but will have the light of life' for the first time. It is an active sentence – of following and walking, and even the light is the light of life.

It is easier to walk forward, into new life, when we can see the way.

This lens of the law is no guarantee of good seeing and good judging. Jesus goes on to lay down the opportunity to judge – it is worth noting how often he does so in the gospels.

'You judge by human standards; I judge no one.' Instead he sees, clearly and compassionately, and shines a light into the hearts of those who would throw stones, and the woman who would suffer under them. Maybe, some there could now see enough to take a step into the light.

> In him was life, and the life was the light of all people. The light shines in the darkness, and the darkness did not overcome it.
> JOHN 1:4–5

Jesus heals a man born blind

This incident (see John 9:1–12) begins with more of the same – questions of sin and judgement – and it is the disciples who are caught up in this way of seeing.

> Judging others makes us blind, whereas love is illuminating. By judging others, we blind ourselves to our own evil and to the grace which others are just as entitled to as we are.[8]

Once again, the person concerned is talked over – an object lesson in a discussion about sinfulness. Was it this man, or his parents, who got what they deserved? You can see the appeal of this way of thinking. It feels just, but it can easily slide into a feeling of superiority if we aren't suffering ourselves. It allows us to think that those who are suffering in some way deserve it. It leaves little room for compassion or action for justice. All of us encounter pain and difficulties in our lives and, when we do, the cruelty of this view can become an obstacle between us and God.

What must the man born blind have thought as he listened to this talk?

'Neither this man nor his parents sinned; he was born blind so that God's works might be revealed in him,' Jesus responds (9:3).

Jesus did not go looking for sin and guilt, and did not apportion blame. Human pain is, rather, the place where God's work is to be done. This seems to fit in with the pattern we see in the gospels, and also in our own lives. Bad things happen; good people and bad people alike suffer (the psalmist seems particularly offended by this, and it is the theme of the book of Job); but God seems to specialise in the transformation of bad things. It is the resurrection power, to redeem, restore, make new. What is more, it seems that the work is not God's alone: 'We must work the works of him who sent me while it is day; night is coming when no one can work' (9:4). There is a 'we' in that sentence – *we* must work God's works. So the challenge is not to judge, but to join in with God's work. God longs for us to act, as partners. What an extraordinary thought! The hope is that when we are in hopeless and most desperate situations, like the man born blind, like the woman, we can encounter the glory and mercy of God. We are open to the possibility of transformation. Once again, Jesus' language is full of action. 'Work' is the key repeated word.

There is a shadow at the edge of this glory, though – night is coming.

'Night is coming when no one can work. As long as I am in the world, I am the light of the world.' This great 'I am' saying, 'the light of the world', is overshadowed by Jesus' knowledge that he is on a path that will lead to deep darkness, to death. He works, not ignoring the coming night, but in defiance of it.

A brief excursion into darkness[9]

Sometimes, it seems that the Christian life must be light and bright and sunny, that it must be activity and busyness and cheerfulness. But sometimes, all that brightness can give us a headache. Darkness is not in itself a bad thing. The night brings its own gifts, hard as they may be to receive. It seems that perhaps what makes a mystic is one who is given the capacity to sit through the 'dark night of the soul',[10] and has come to see that darkness is not dark to God (Psalm 139:12). Sometimes, when we can no longer rely on our eyes, we can see that more clearly. When we find ourselves in dark times, we can remember the nights Jesus spent awake in prayer. He faced the darkness of the temptations, the darkness of Gethsemane, the darkness that fell over the cross, the darkness of the tomb before dawn. He has been before us into the dark. Perhaps, even there, we can draw closer to God. The great work of medieval mysticism, *The Cloud of Unknowing*,[11] explores God who is beyond knowing in the clear light of reason and certainty, but who is not beyond loving. It encourages us to be patient in the dark, in the cloud, for it is there we find God.

God often speaks to people in their dreams and offers companionship in the lions' den. The night simply is. It is part of our lives. Without it, we would be poorer. It is worth remembering its richness, its beauty, its capacity to draw us to God, as we proceed. The imagery in scripture is multilayered.

Sight

Night is coming for Jesus, yet this is his response – to give sight to the blind. We act now to lift the darkness we can. We work while it is light. This theme emerges again in the story of the raising of Lazarus (11:4, 9–16). Light and work go together – and the work is the transformation of suffering and death, sin and despair, into hope and life. It is the bursting out of a new dawn, a new light to live by. This is the life-light in action: the glory-light that is found in the strangest places.

Glory is found, too, in mud.

This is the work that Jesus did – spitting on the ground, making mud and smearing it on the eyes of the one born blind. Here again, we may well have an echo of the Hebrew origin stories, of the creation of the first human, whose name is a play on the Hebrew word for human – *ha'adam*, and also for dust or earth – *adamah*.[12]

> Then the Lord God formed man from the dust of the ground and breathed into his nostrils the breath of life; and the man became a living being.
>
> GENESIS 2:7

This smearing on of mud seems a prophetic act, a sign of the new creation. Perhaps it speaks of a time when the old way of looking at things no longer applies, when the human's eyes are recreated.

Then, the man with mud-smeared eyes is sent to the 'pool of the sent', the pool of Siloam. It must have been a challenging walk, and a rather remarkable act of faith, to go alone on the basis of this slight conversation. This man is no longer an object lesson in punishment for sin: he is now one for faith, who sets off to find the unseen pool in obedience to a voice.

But first, a little about this pool. It was the pool the pilgrims washed in on the way to the temple, so it was a pool of cleansing, of preparation for worship. It was more than that, though; it was the pool from which the priest went to draw water for the offering during the Feast of Tabernacles. This was the only major celebration involving an offering of water, and it was during this that Jesus had just declared himself to be the one who quenches our thirst, the source of living water that can bubble up within us, and overflow from us (7:37–39).

The blind man would have been excluded from the celebrations by reason of his blindness, as the law required – here, at this pool, he finds a reason to celebrate. A hunt through the Hebrew scriptures for 'Siloam' or 'Shiloah', the older pronunciation, reveals a connection with the messianic new order, new age. In Isaiah 8:6, the people do not accept 'the gentle waters of Shiloah'. This man does. This man washes the mud away from his eyes, and comes back seeing, much to the bewilderment of his neighbours. They do not know who he is any more. His identity is no longer 'the man born blind' – he is the man who received his sight. He is a new creation.

The uproar that follows brings him before the religious leaders, who are still arguing about sin and judgement and who is right. Here, it is ridiculous as well as destructive. A life-changing, powerfully good, extraordinary thing has happened, and the religious leaders are overlooking it – seeing it as sabbath-breaking. It is clear how stuck in their seeing the religious people are. They do not see the revelation of the glory of God; they see law and its breaking.

But look what happens next. The man who can now see is thrown out of the synagogue, and Jesus goes to find him. Like the good shepherd from Luke's parable (Luke 15:1–7), Jesus goes to find the one who is lost – who is regarded as lost. The man who can now see has never seen Jesus, but he has heard his voice. As Jesus speaks to him here, he seems to recognise the voice, and he believes. In his place of need, rejection and gratitude, his eyes and ears are open, and he is able to respond to the gift before him. This is how the grace of God works. It is offered freely to us, poured out, 'for from his fullness we have all received, grace upon grace' (John 1:16).

And Jesus, clearly within the hearing of the Pharisees, does talk about judgement now, but in the context of seeing. It seems the judgement he speaks of liberates those who know they are blind; those who think they can see but do not are in a worse position.

> Your eye is the lamp of your body. When your eyes are healthy, your whole body is full of light. But if it is not healthy, your body is full of darkness. Therefore consider whether the light in you is not darkness. If then your whole body is full of light, and no part of it in darkness, it will be as full of light as when a lamp gives you light with its rays.
> LUKE 11:34–36

This is the worst sort of blindness – blindness which thinks it is clear sight, for which there is no hope. It is a powerful lesson for us all. We need to remain humble. We keep trusting in God. We seek to learn from Jesus, who opens the eyes of the blind.

The man who has been thrown out of his fellowship has true sight. He has encountered Jesus, and his life has been thrown open to the light of life. For here is an astonishing truth: in Matthew's gospel, Jesus says that *we* are the light of the world.

> You are the light of the world. A city built on a hill cannot be hidden. No one after lighting a lamp puts it under the bushel basket, but on the lampstand, and it gives light to all in the house. In the same way, let your light shine before others, so that they may see your good works and give glory to your Father in heaven.
>
> MATTHEW 5:14–17

The thought that we could participate in such glory can be exhilarating, but may not be good for us. It may lead us into the temptation of thinking we have more sight than we do, into the temptation of the Pharisees. Or, knowing our limitations, it can make us uneasy, that the torch has been placed in our hands and we doubt we can carry it. Jesus does not say that we must be the light of the world, but that we are. It is not a condition, or a command.

The light is not always comfortable. Bringing things into the light can be difficult and dangerous work, both in our own lives and in society. Maybe that is another reason why discussion of light is coupled with warnings against judgement. If we feel we have light, we can feel entitled, obliged maybe, to judge others. While discerning is wise to keep ourselves safe, and to avoid falling into wrongdoing ourselves, this light Jesus speaks of seems to be the light of mercy and goodness, of life and joy. With gentleness, we can let God's light illuminate a dark situation, and let that light do its work. Rather than a harsh and unforgiving spotlight, this light is more like spring sunshine, 'a light so lovely it draws people'.[13] We grow towards it, and the light will reveal what is hidden in the darkness. Maybe, for now, that is enough. Maybe any more, and we risk throwing out the man born blind.

Could we, too, be a life-giving light? Perhaps we can participate in the glory of God, when goodness and love and gratitude flow through us, where we shine like the broken pieces of glass, throwing colour and beauty and light into the lives of those around. There was a lamp in the temple that never went out, the lamp of the presence of God.

What if that is the lamp that shines in our own broken hearts?

Could we respond to the call to be part of the light to lighten the nations, to shine this life-light, this God-glory, this goodness and love and joy and forgiveness, this justice and mercy, wherever we go?

A lamp on a stand – a help and a hope in the darkness.

> The true light, which enlightens everyone, *has come* into the world.
>
> JOHN 1:9 (altered)

Reflection and response

Study

John 9:1–5

- What do you think of the disciples' question, and Jesus' answer?
- How did Jesus respond to the blind man?
- Recall some times when you encountered someone in need. How did you feel? What happened?
- Think of a time when you were in need. How did you feel? What happened?
- What kind of work might Jesus be meaning here?

John 9:6–7

- Why do you think Jesus made mud, and sent him away to be healed at the pool of Siloam?

John 9:8–16

- This sign provoked a response. How would you describe it? Why did it do so?
- What do you understand Jesus' attitude to the sabbath to be?
- Are there ways in which we might be missing the 'main thing'?

John 9:35–41

- Jesus went to find the healed man. Have you ever experienced rejection? Did anyone come to find you?
- Can we find ways of reaching out to people who have been hurt by the church in the past? (See further reading: *Sowing, Reaping, Keeping*.)

Further study

Matthew 6:19–24

- At the core of this passage are treasure, the heart and seeing. Take some time to think about the eye as the lamp of the body.
- What might that mean for you?
- Why do you think Jesus spoke of it in this context?

Acts 9:1–19 (the conversion of Saul)

- How might thinking of Jesus as light of the world, and of his teaching on the eyes and seeing, help us with this passage?

Revelation 21:22–26 (the light in the new Jerusalem)

- Meditate on this vision, and look out for signs of it appearing.

Genesis 1 and John 1

- Read these two passages, and notice the ways in which John draws on the ancient Hebrew story. Hold the ideas of light and life in your mind, and notice how they develop.

Prayer and meditation

A prayer for the opening of eyes (to be said throughout the day)
May I see signs of your kingdom springing up like seeds, working like yeast in the dough.

Candle prayer

When I led an Advent retreat, we considered Jesus, the light of the world, as the light was failing. We then lit a tall candle. Each person had a tea light, some had Christingles from the cathedral service earlier that day, and from one small flame in the dark we filled the room with light. Some lit their candle from the central one, some passed the light on to their neighbours. Whether you are alone, or with others, spreading the light like this reminds us of some powerful truths.

So, have a number of candles, and matches, available – enough for one each if there are more than one of you. Make the place as dark as you can, and light the first candle. Here are some suggestions for words you could say:

- The light shines in the darkness, and the darkness did not overcome it (1:5).
- The true light, which enlightens everyone, was coming into the world (1:9).
- And we have seen his glory, the glory as of a father's only son, full of grace and truth (1:14).
- From his fullness we have all received, grace upon grace (1:16).
- No one has ever seen God. It is God the only Son, who is close to the Father's heart, who has made him known (1:18).
- I am the light of the world. Whoever follows me will never walk in darkness but will have the light of life (8:12).

Then, spread the light from the main candle until all are shining. Here are some more words that you might like to use:

May we bring the light of Christ to those in darkness,
may we chase away the shadows with hope and love,
may we hold a lamp for feet that stumble,
may we too be lights in the world.

Oh, God, who spoke and light came into being, may we forever dwell in the brightness of knowing you.

Quaker light meditation[14]
The light of love and grace transforms our seeing.

The Society of Friends have various pamphlets available to help introduce the practices of meditation and silent prayer. These are usually undertaken together, as a group, and the meditation below can be done alone or with others. The words in inverted commas are those of George Fox, founder of the Quaker movement (1624–91). Many of the others are a paraphrase. Again, you may wish to begin this in darkness, or use a small light as a focus.

1. **Look inside.** 'Your teacher is within you. Mind what is pure in you to guide you to God' – remember the work of the Spirit within you.

2. **Identify the light.** 'Now this is the Light with which you are lighted, which shows you when you do wrong.' When you bring yourself into the light, you see your troubles, your temptations and your wrongdoings.

3. **Let the light show you yourself.** 'Mind the pure light of God in you' which shows the things in you that are not light: let your conscience be stirred. Let the light of Jesus Christ search you. Do not be afraid. It is the light of love.

4. **Trace the light to its source.** Stand in God's counsel, learn from the lights that 'you may be led forth in his life and likeness'. God is restoring his image in you.

5 **Trust the light to show you the alternative.** Have courage to stand still in the light: it is the light of your Saviour. If you look at your sin, you are swallowed up in it, so look to the light by which you see it instead, and let your focus be on the source.

6 **Feel the new life grow.** 'He who follows the light comes to have the light of life.' The Lord has sown a seed in you that lies shut up in the darkness, with winter storms about it. He sends his light to the seed, that with time the new life will grow.

7 **See other people in the light.** 'As you abide in the light, the life-light, you will see the kinship that is amongst you, for in the light no self-will, no mastery can stand.' We are all equal before the light.

8 **See the world in the light.** This light lets you see all the world as it is, and keeps you mindful of God.

9 **Learn to love in the light.** Standing in the eternal power and light of God, we have strength to love those who persecute and wrong us; we have light enough to shed light on the paths of those who are against us. This is how we learn to love.

On darkness

Pick one of the verses from the 'Candle prayer' section, or from below, and memorise it. (You could search a concordance for 'darkness' and find others.) Hold it in your mind as you find or make a dark place.

Spend time in the dark. Notice other sources of light – a streetlight, a neighbour's garden lamps, a passing car. Quieten into the darkness, holding the verse in your mind, or say it out loud.

- Indeed, you are my lamp, O Lord, the Lord lightens my darkness (2 Samuel 22:29).
- He uncovers the deeps out of darkness, and brings deep darkness to light (Job 12:22).

- Yet I am not silenced by the darkness, by the thick darkness that covers my face (Job 23:17, NIV).
- If I say, 'Surely the darkness shall cover me, and the light about me become night', even the darkness is not dark to you; the night is bright as the day, for darkness is as light to you (Psalm 139:11–12).

It is important to acknowledge the darkness we find ourselves in at times. Important growth happens in winter seasons. Acknowledge hard things, if you can, before God. You can either light a candle/turn on a lamp, or continue to sit in the dark.

Reflect on sources of light that reached into your darkness. Remember times when you have been helped in difficulty, when light has reached you, and give thanks.

Consider if there are ways you could lighten the darkness of another.

End with: 'Jesus says, "I am the light of the world."'

We walk best when we can see the way, but sometimes we need to take a step, and find there is light for the path.

Creative response

> Not knowing when the dawn will come, I open every door.
> Emily Dickinson[15]

Photography, light writing

Why not take on a photography project? You could aim to photograph one of the below every day for a week, or simply take a camera/ phone with you wherever you go and see what you find.

- Light sources in your home/community.
- Reflections and light affecting the same object or view at different times, in different light.
- The same subject using various filters.

You could print off any you like, to pin up or to make into 'sending you light' cards.

Tea-light jam jars

Use jam jars to make tea-light holders.

On plain tissue, use felt-tip pens to colour designs or patterns. Perhaps add water to the pens for a more fluid effect. You could also add words. Use this to line a jam jar.

Alternatively, use scraps of differently coloured tissue paper and glue to line your jam jar. You could use this time to pray for those who feel broken and rejected, and pray over the broken and rejected parts of your own self and story. Make something beautiful!

If you wanted to use thick paper, you could make patterns or shapes in the paper using a hole punch or craft knife, so light will shine through in some places. You could write a verse in light.

Black and white pictures

Use charcoal and white paper, then chalk or white pastel and black paper, to draw the same subject. What do you notice, using the two techniques?

Life and service

Darkness

Experiment with doing something in the dark, aware of safety. What do you notice?

Prayer walking

Are there dark places in your neighbourhood – figurative and literal? Do a prayer walk with others, asking God's light to break in. Or pray at home, using a map.

Sunlight

Consider solar power for a device, a renewable electricity supplier, drying things outside if you can. Use the light of the sun.

Grow seeds, perhaps cress. Do they need time in the dark? Notice how they turn towards light. How does that apply to you?

Social media

Think about the arguments in these chapters, and compare them to those you encounter on social media and comments sections online. How can we respond in a way which is more like Jesus? How can we be light in this particular dark place?

A light that shines in the darkness

Can you join a campaign to highlight an injustice you care about; shine a light on unjust behaviour; or stand up for someone who has been excluded? Such action can be risky, and is best done thoughtfully, prayerfully and with others.

Social media enables individuals and groups to alert others to the unethical behaviour of companies and governments. So check the facts, and see if you can make a difference.

If you have been prayer walking in dark places, perhaps you can contact local politicians and community groups to join in making it better. Perhaps there is a need for street pastors in your community.

If you know someone with sight difficulties, talk to them about their experience. Ask what you can do to help.

Find out more about living with visual impairment.

Further reading

Seamus Heaney's translation of St John of the Cross, 'Song of the soul that rejoices in knowing God through faith', incorporated into an original work 'Station Island' from Heaney's collection *Opened Ground, 1966–96* (Faber and Faber, 1998)
Søren Kierkegaard, *The Sickness Unto Death* (Penguin Classics, 1986)
Richard Rohr, *The Naked Now* (Crossroad, 2009)
Laurence Singlehurst, *Sowing, Reaping, Keeping* (IVP, 1995)
A. Spearing (ed.), *The Cloud of Unknowing* (Penguin, 2001)
Barbara Brown Taylor, *Learning to Walk in the Dark* (HarperCollins, 2014)

5

I am the good shepherd, I am the gate for the sheep

'Very truly, I tell you, anyone who does not enter the sheepfold by the gate but climbs in by another way is a thief and a bandit. The one who enters by the gate is the shepherd of the sheep. The gatekeeper opens the gate for him, and the sheep hear his voice. He calls his own sheep by name and leads them out. When he has brought out all his own, he goes ahead of them, and the sheep follow him because they know his voice. They will not follow a stranger, but they will run from him because they do not know the voice of strangers.' Jesus used this figure of speech with them, but they did not understand what he was saying to them.

So again Jesus said to them, 'Very truly, I tell you, I am the gate for the sheep. All who came before me are thieves and bandits; but the sheep did not listen to them. I am the gate. Whoever enters by me will be saved, and will come in and go out and find pasture. The thief comes only to steal and kill and destroy. I came that they may have life, and have it abundantly.

'I am the good shepherd. The good shepherd lays down his life for the sheep. The hired hand, who is not the shepherd and does not own the sheep, sees the wolf coming and leaves the sheep and runs away – and the wolf snatches them and scatters them. The hired hand runs away because a hired hand does not care for the sheep. I am the good shepherd. I know my own and my own know me, just as the Father knows me and I know the Father. And I lay down my life for the sheep. I have other sheep that do not belong to this fold.

I must bring them also, and they will listen to my voice. So there will be one flock, one shepherd. For this reason the Father loves me, because I lay down my life in order to take it up again. No one takes it from me, but I lay it down of my own accord. I have power to lay it down, and I have power to take it up again. I have received this command from my Father.'

JOHN 10:1–18

The good shepherd

Hidden away in the darkness of the catacombs under the streets of Rome, we find some of the earliest images and symbols used by followers of the Way, of Jesus. The good shepherd, a young clean-shaven man with a lamb across his shoulders, classically dressed and posed, is seen again and again.[16] It is an image that must have spoken powerfully to these early, persecuted Christians. Up to our own time, David's song of the shepherd (Psalm 23) has helped and sustained people through their own valley of shadows. Many know it by heart. It remains the most often-chosen reading at funerals.

Of all the images, of all the 'I am' sayings, why do we respond so powerfully to the good shepherd? Let us explore our text, and see what we find.

Questions, answers and a shifting story

This saying follows on from the one before – 'I am the light of the world'. The setting, as we saw in the previous chapter, is the Feast of Tabernacles. The atmosphere is hostile, argumentative, challenging to Jesus. The religious leaders raise questions of sin and judgement, of identity and authority. Who is Jesus anyway, that he says and does these things?

This good shepherd story is an answer to these questions and challenges that have been rolling on over several chapters of our reading. Jesus often responds to questioning with a story. Stories speak to the whole person, not simply the arguing mind. Jesus does not join in the debate on the terms of his opponents, with a kind of rhetorical tennis, batting ideas back and forth. Those conversations tend to entrench, rather than open up, people's thinking. Jesus presents his listeners with a whole new frame, a whole new way of seeing things, which draws on lived experience and our heart's response.

We are so accustomed to seeing the good shepherd as a comfort that it can be easy for us to miss the sting in this story – and we will look at both that sting, and the comfort. Jesus has a double audience. There is the man who received his sight, and others outside the synagogue, and also the religious leaders who threw him out. That second group would have been stung by this story, the first, strengthened and encouraged.

As Jesus tells the story, he shifts focus several times, giving different perspectives. We are unsure where we will settle – with the robber, the gatekeeper, the shepherd, the gate, the sheep? As he shifts the narrative voice, we see Jesus' capacity to examine the same thing from different perspectives, to see other points of view. In telling the story this way, he unsettles his listeners, perhaps confusing them, but also enabling them to jump from their own fixed viewpoint and see afresh.

He starts the story with the negative – with the thief, the bandit, climbing in over the wall. It is a stern answer to the religious leaders, the Pharisees. The emotional drive for this story seems to be compassion for the man who can now see, and outrage at his treatment by the religious gatekeepers. This compassion and outrage are coupled with a deep knowledge of the Hebrew scriptures, for these words have a whole hinterland behind them. Those who heard would know what he meant.

Ezekiel and the shepherds

Ezekiel 34 begins emphatically: 'The word of the Lord came to me: Mortal, prophesy against the shepherds of Israel.'

Ezekiel was from a priestly family, who had been taken into exile in Babylon as a young man – he might number himself among the shepherds. The shepherds in his prophecy, however, are doing a terrible job. They are exploiting their position and their flock, neglecting their sheep. Reading this passage through while remembering the Pharisees' treatment of the man born blind, you can feel it sting.

> You have not strengthened the weak, you have not healed the sick, you have not bound up the injured, you have not brought back the strayed, you have not sought the lost, but with force and harshness you have ruled them.
>
> EZEKIEL 34:4

Jesus clearly draws on a shared knowledge of this prophecy to confront those who challenged him. They know that the prophecy continues, saying that God himself will search for the sheep, as Jesus searched for the one who can now see. God will gather those who are lost and scattered, and will feed them with good pasture. God will be their shepherd, will bind up the injured, will strengthen the weak. They will be fed with justice. And Jesus claims this role, the role of the good shepherd, for himself.

When we can be cared for by God, the power and importance of human leaders – tyrants, emperors, Pharisees – is hugely diminished. And it sets a high bar for those human leaders, those who would be a shepherd of a flock. That nourishing, self-giving, gentle leading of the good shepherd is our standard. For those of us with responsibilities for and influence over the welfare of others – and that is just about all of us – meditating on the good shepherd is a useful and humbling experience.

In Ezekiel's prophecy, the flock are not spared the shepherd's scrutiny, loved and cared for as they are (34:17–22). We too are capable of self-interested cruelty. We can muddy the clear waters for each other and trample the pasture. We can push weaker sheep out of the way and overlook the needs of others until they are scattered. It is not just the shepherds who need to model their care on the good shepherd. The flock is interdependent; we can all look out for each other's welfare, seek to protect and be gentle with the weak. In fact, with a diminished importance placed on human leaders, our communal life together becomes all the more central. Once again, we see that God cares greatly about how we treat each other – especially how we treat those weaker than ourselves.

The shepherd king and the shepherd prophet

The Ezekiel passage refers back to David, who was looking after the sheep in the fields around Bethlehem when he was anointed king (1 Samuel 16). The prophets who lived long after David look both back and forward. They look back to his reign as a golden age, with a *hiraeth* as the Welsh say – a melancholy, homesick longing. They look forward to a time when such a king will rule again. The messiah would be from the line of David – a good shepherd.

The other words that Jesus draws on in his telling of the good shepherd are found in Psalm 23, David's most famous poem. It is believed he wrote it near the end of his life, looking back on years of both victory and heartbreak, and back further to the days when he guarded his father's flocks. These are words that have given strength, courage and hope to many. We will not always find ourselves in gentle water-meadows, but we know that the shepherd will be with us even in the darkest valley. We will not be forsaken, lost and alone. We need not be afraid.

The valley of the shadow is not a place we can linger. It is a place we will walk through, though, and it is good advice to keep moving, to not set up camp, to trust that at the end of this will be a table spread.

It is worth mulling over what it might mean to dwell in the house of the Lord our whole lives long (Psalm 23:6). To take the presence, the provision, the comfort and the rest of God with us, aware of it surrounding us whether we are in green pastures or the dark valley, that is *shalom* indeed. Wholehearted peace.

Of course, there are even earlier stories of a shepherd leader: Moses – first prince of Egypt, then shepherd of Jethro's flocks. It is to Moses the shepherd that God is revealed as the 'I am', the name spoken out of the flames of the burning bush. And Moses the shepherd has the task of leading the people across that wilderness, of working with God to find water, food and places to camp. For generations, people's everyday experience of shepherds would have rung with all this meaning.

Jesus, the shepherd and the gate

So, when Jesus began to talk about shepherds and flocks, the words would have called forth a rich vein of memory and association. They would have carried real weight for Jesus' hearers.

We have already met the thieves and robbers who are climbing over the walls to steal and to use the flock for their own advantage, in the first line of this story. Then comes the shepherd, entering by the gate, calling out his own flock by name, and leading them out. Sheepfolds were stone enclosures common to several shepherds. Middle-Eastern shepherds did not harry and chase their sheep, rather they named them, called the sheep out by name, and the sheep followed the one they recognised.

It is possible that Jesus is picking up a detail from the story of the one who received his sight in the previous chapter. When Jesus healed him, he did not know what Jesus looked like – he heard, rather than saw, that encounter. The voice told him to go and wash, and he did. When Jesus found him again after he had been thrown out of the synagogue, this man did not recognise Jesus by sight, but he seems to have recognised his voice, and is ready to once again follow. Perhaps it is not too fanciful to suppose that Jesus was drawing on a contrast – the voices that threw him out, the voice that restored him – in thinking about the voice of the good shepherd.

Knowing the voice: an illustration

Of course, knowing the voice, and distinguishing it from the voices of those who would lead us to harm, is no easy thing. I think it helps to come to a place where we don't see the path ahead of us as a narrow tightrope – one false move and we are lost – but that we look for the relationship, and recognise the freedom to walk behind the shepherd, listening for the voice.

My husband and I stayed in a tiny National Trust cottage by the Thames at Buscot, arriving on a grey October afternoon. A little way along the footpath was the parish church, St Mary's. I had been looking forward to seeing it, having heard there was an original Burne Jones stained-glass window there. Despite the failing light, we went. The church was open. When we entered, and looked around, we saw that every window was full of lovely glass in Burne Jones' style. The same detailed carpet of flowers, the same pale faces with shadowed eyes. Maybe this one was it, or that one…

And then we went up to the front of the church, and saw the glass above the table, darkening in the east. I had no doubt, the moment I saw it, that this was the one. It lacked many of the identifiable stylistic qualities of the others. There was no tapestry of flowers, no angled, pale faces. It was a figure of a young man in white toga over a red tunic – Roman dress – with a white lamb over his shoulders. He was standing in a landscape we would discover when we walked the next day – the landscape outside the church. The brown Thames snaked behind him; his feet were on the water; the trees and the vegetation and even the sky were the very same. What I thought when I saw this window was – if there is a piece of art here done by a master, then this, undoubtedly, is it. It was moving, powerful. It had a depth that went beyond style-matching familiarity. It was a picture you could look at for hours, and let it speak to you and bring you comfort; a picture that could give you courage and strength for the day. As I looked at it, I thought about knowing the voice, recognising the authentic voice of Jesus as we walk by our own rivers, looking at the sky above. That voice will have such vision, such life about it. It will be a 'match' in a deeper way than stylistic similarity. It will have authentic life.

It is not always easy, identifying the authentic voice of the shepherd. History is full of the mistakes people have made, thinking they are doing the right thing but going terribly wrong. I do not see us going so wrong when we seek to follow the way of love, seeking to keep our eyes fixed on Jesus, and learning from him.

We can see in this story how radical Jesus' approach is. We can see how he reaches out, as a shepherd does, caring for the lost and the hurting. We can see the emphasis on love, and living out a life of love. We can see how he offers forgiveness, how he subverts argument with creative storytelling, how the ways of peace matter – as does justice. We can learn in our own lives, by our own rivers, under our own skies, to see the marks of God in our own lives and those of others – compassion and gratitude and self-sacrifice. We can see new shoots of the kingdom – but we do have to learn to look, to accustom our eyes to see, to expect to see.

The gate, the meadow and abundant life

There is a twofold task that Jesus undertakes for us. One is to keep us safe, to be the gate. The other is to lead us out. In the ancient Near East, there was no wooden gate. The shepherd would lie across the gap in the circular sheepfold at night, protecting the sheep both from wild animals and sheep-rustlers. Jesus keeps the sheep safe.

Sometimes, the Christian life can feel all about keeping safe. It can feel all about avoiding sin and temptation, avoiding the dangers that are 'out there', staying safe in churches. A sheepfold, where the sheep are kept all the time, will become a very unsavoury, smelly place. The grass won't last long, and the sheep will become hungry and unwell. Safety does not consist in keeping away from an 'unholy' world, but from being with the shepherd.

We need safety and refuge. We need sanctuary. We need to lie down and sleep in safety. And then, as the shepherd gets to his feet and calls us out of the fold, we need to continue to find our safety in the presence of the shepherd as we step out into the new light of morning.

If God made the world, and all things hold together in Christ, we know that the shepherd knows what he is doing when he leads us out. He knows about the dark valley, and will not abandon us there, but it is not all dark valley. It is also green pasture, flowing water and the kingdom coming on earth as in heaven. Abundant life is such a marvellous promise: a life of depth and beauty, of love and mercy, of peace and justice, of compassion, forgiveness and reconciliation – these are some of the signs of abundant life. It is not a small, hidden-away life, but life hidden in Christ – a life of faith and adventure: a life of stepping out of the sheepfold and finding that the pastures are green, and the shepherd keeps calling our name.

Safe in Christ, knowing the healing and forgiveness of being safe in Christ, we need not fear. The shepherd watches over the flock.

The shepherd lays down his life

More than that, the shepherd lays down his life for the sheep. The hired hands may run, but Jesus loves the flock and will defend it to the end. He will take on the danger that the sheep face himself, for their sake. He will feel the full force of the wolf. Jesus does not end the story there, with the wolf, at what appears to be a natural ending. His mind continues to expand and open the picture for us – not just these sheep, free to roam in the pasture, but other sheep will also be included – different ones. Most probably we think of Gentile sheep – people from nations other than Israel, also included in the flock. In our own time, we can continue to think of people who we would not expect to be included. Jesus is always calling us to expand our vision, to take a further imaginative step, to see God's vision of one flock and one shepherd. We see, too, that this laying down of life is something Jesus does in obedience to the Father. John's initial audience, knowing how the story goes, would have felt the power of these words, and held them in mind as the story continued to unfold, and we can too, as we walk on to Lazarus' tomb, just outside Jerusalem.

Both good shepherd and lamb

When we say 'good shepherd', we can remember that the word we translate 'good' does not carry a meaning of cold personal morality, but it is a word we sometimes render 'beautiful'. It is a word of delight, attractiveness, a radiant and life-full goodness – to follow such a shepherd is no hardship. To follow a shepherd who takes on the fiercest wolf on my behalf is also a cause for rejoicing. We also remember that John the Baptist, at the beginning of the gospel, greets Jesus like this:

> Here is the Lamb of God who takes away the sin of the world!
> JOHN 1:29

Jesus, too, is the lamb. He was obedient even to death. He is both shepherd, dying defending the flock, and lamb, dying in place of it. He takes on the very worst that can be done and, by going through it, exhausts and empties the power of death and destruction and evil. That changes everything.

And, also, by being both the shepherd and the lamb, the one who leads and the one who gives himself up, we see again that model of flow Jesus tries to help his followers understand again and again. There is a love and mutuality between the Father and the Son, and as it is with them, so we, too, are invited into this mutually self-giving and affirming love. Within this pattern, this dance, we can in time begin to see what Jesus might be meaning, what this life he is calling us to might be like; and we find in his example the courage to trust and to follow, knowing that it is the beautiful shepherd who leads us. He has gone before us. Wherever we are, the shepherd is there, walking by our side.

Reflection and response

Study

John 10:1–2, 6–10

- What do you think Jesus means when he speaks of thieves and robbers, taking and spoiling (compare verse 1 with the imagery in the other verses)? Have you encountered people or situations that have left you feeling robbed?
- What do you think of verse 10?

John 10:3–5

- How do we hear the voice of Jesus? Have you had experience of this? What happens if we don't experience anything that we could call 'hearing the voice'? Are there different ways you feel you hear from God?
- Are there other voices that confuse us?
- Have you had times when you felt you had freedom in Jesus, or times when it felt like you had specific guidance? What were those experiences like?
- What does it mean to be called by name? What difference does it make when people know you by name and address you by name?
- Do you have a sense of being known by God? What is that like?

- Why do you think the Pharisees did not understand the figure of speech (v. 6)? Why do you think Jesus spoke in such language? Do you notice any changes in the language from verse 7 onwards?
- What do you think they understood by 'the gate'? What does it mean to you?
- Does it help to think of Jesus being a gate for you?
- What do we learn about following the good shepherd from these verses?
- In what parts of your life are you, too, a shepherd?
- How does the thought of being one of Jesus' sheep strike you? Might we have misunderstood what it means to be a sheep?

Further study

Ezekiel 34

- Consider the way the relationship between God and the people is described in this chapter. How do you respond to the description of God's love and care for the flock? Do you feel that includes you? What do we see about how the sheep should behave towards each other?

1 Samuel 16

- How might being a shepherd have helped David be a king?

Exodus 2:11—3:12 (and the rest of the story)

- Did Moses have lessons to learn about leadership? How did his experience as Jethro's shepherd enrich him?

Luke 15:1–7 and Matthew 18:1–15

- What do these parables tell us about being a sheep? In what ways are we shepherds, and how are we at being sheep? What does it mean to follow? What does it mean to trust?

Psalm 23

- See meditation on page 87.

Prayer and meditation

The Lamb at the centre of the throne will be their shepherd, and he will guide them to springs of the water of life.
REVELATION 7:17

Listening to the voice

The fact that I think that I am following your will does not mean that I am actually doing so. But I believe that the desire to please you does in fact please you.
Thomas Merton[17]

Prayer for the beginning of the day:

Good Shepherd, you know what lies before me today.
Help me to hear your voice, and remain close to you.
Guide me beside still waters, keep me at peace.
Nourish me with your presence, let me have enough to give.
Let me follow you this day, and always.

Prayer during the day:

Good Shepherd, let me see you ahead of me,
and know which way to go.

Psalm 23

You may wish to listen to some peaceful, uplifting music as you read the psalm.

Read slowly, imagining yourself into the scene. Most of the lines are in two halves. This style of poetry lends itself to a breath meditation – read one half on the in-breath, the other on the out, if it is comfortable to do so. Slow your breathing. Allow your mind to still. Focus on the images the words conjure up.

Linger by the still waters. Think of times and places that have been still waters for you. Expect to encounter them in your daily walk. Look out for them.

Do the same with good pasture. What feeds and sustains you? What restores you? Look back and remember, with thanks, and look forward with expectation that you will be fed and restored again. Allow your soul to be restored. Allow God to bless you and lift you up. Be lifted up. Know that God carries the lambs, binds up the injured, protects the weak.

Look for the good things that are spread today on your table. Ask yourself, what does it mean for me to thrive?

Pray

> Dear Lord, we pray for those who have suffered at the hands of bad shepherds. We pray that you will restore what has been taken from them, that they will receive protection, and justice. We pray that they will find hope and healing in you, and that you will be a good shepherd to them. We pray they may have abundant life. Amen

Creative response

Writing

You might like to write down your own response to, or version of, Psalm 23. Mine is at the end of the chapter.

Still waters

You might like to make small cards, or have photos on your phone or laptop, to remind you of still waters, to encourage your soul to lie down and rest in God during the day. Look out for such still waters. Alternatively, you could place them by doorways you pass through, remembering that Jesus is your gate. Use words from the readings to remind you. Know that the shepherd is going ahead of you.

Lord, let me trust in your leading, let me rest in you.
Amen

Called by name

Jesus says he knows the sheep by name. What is it like when someone uses your name? What does that say about your relationship? Maybe, in prayer, you can imagine Jesus calling you by name. You might like to read Isaiah 43:1–4, John 20:11–18 or John 1:43–51. What is it like to be sought out and personally invited to follow Jesus?

You might like to hold a stone, or a piece of broken pot, carefully in your hand as you pray. Feel the weight and form of it. Look at its unique properties. Do they say anything to you? Then, write your name on one side, and 'Jesus' on the other. Use it to remember that you have been called by name. I have a flint in my pocket. Feeling its edges helps.

Wolves

If the question about robbers in the Bible study section was relevant to you, you might wish to give some thought to wolves. Who are, or have been, the wolves in your life? Have you experienced bad shepherds? Do you need to talk to someone about your experience? Do you need to seek justice, recovery, forgiveness?

Doorways and gateways

'Threshold times' are times when one thing is ending but the next is yet to be established. It can be a very uncomfortable time. Liminal space forces us to be open to new possibilities, to listen and watch for hints, clues, guidance, a way forward. Learning to be more at ease with uncertainty is one of the lessons of this time. Courage to face it, too.

You might like to choose one of the following creative responses:

Writing. Write the story of times of major change in your life, summarised in doors you passed through – doors that opened and closed. You might wish to include symbolic rites of passage, too, especially ones related to your faith journey. What changed? How did you face the in-between times? Was Jesus a gate for you?

Drawing. Choose a door you pass through often, and draw as detailed a picture of it as you can. As you draw, pray for the times you pass through. Are you going out to good pasture? Still water? Or is it more the valley of the shadow? Use the reading, and Psalm 23, to reflect on your daily experience.

Photography. Take pictures of doorways you encounter and pass through. Use them as prayer prompts – for the people and businesses behind them, for the life that flows around your community.

Mythical doorways. Perhaps you can think of doorways, portals, etc. in films and books that have meant something to you, for example Narnia's wardrobe, the doorways in *The Lord of the Rings*, the entrance to Elidor, ways to other dimensions in science fiction and games. What do they tell us about the possibilities in everyday life, the chances and opportunities that a different turn can take? As you go about your day, be on the lookout for doorways that spark your imagination. Write or draw what they spark in you.

Jesus as the gate

If we read this passage again, this time thinking of the cross, we find that this is rich and helpful. We can think of Jesus as the gate, Jesus as the one who lays down his life for the flock, the one who stands between the flock and the wolf, the one who takes the violence and danger instead.

We can think of other doorways and gateways which are involved in the story of the cross – of the blood on the door at Passover (Exodus 12:7) or the curtain in the temple.

Read Matthew 27:45–51. This curtain was huge and heavy. It screened off the holiest place from view. This was where the presence of God was believed to be. Take some time to recognise the presence of God, knowing the barrier is no more, that God is everywhere. Give thanks for Jesus laying down his life for the flock. Give thanks that the gate has been opened.

Life and service

Other sheep from other sheepfolds

Are there ways you can become more involved in the wider church in your area? Are there joint projects you could participate in, services you could attend? Seek to understand more about people outside your own tradition. You could expand that to finding out more about people of other faiths, people of peace, in your area.

What do you understand by Jesus' words: 'one flock, one shepherd'? How can we live so it becomes more true?

Good shepherd

Write down ways in which you have some leadership and/or influence with others. Each of our lives touches others; we all make ripples in our ponds.

Ask God to help you learn to be a good shepherd in these situations, and to follow the good shepherd.

Write down any action or insight that comes to you. Resolve to follow it this week.

Listen/hear

Remember a time when you felt really listened to, and a time when you did not. What was the impact of both occasions? Resolve to be a more attentive listener this week. Give your full attention to whoever is talking to you. Seek to understand them, really hear them, rather than putting your own point of view across.

Poem based on Psalm 23

My pasture is green.
My small world, cupped in
his hand, grows.
Today, shadows are
soft, and the sun
shimmers on clear waters.
Apple blossom
swells in the bud.
I rest in the hollow of
his palm.

Further reading

Michael Mitton, *A Heart to Listen* (BRF, 2004)
Henri Nouwen, *The Return of the Prodigal Son* (DLT, 1992)

6

I am the resurrection and the life

When Jesus arrived, he found that Lazarus had already been in the tomb for four days... When Martha heard that Jesus was coming, she went and met him, while Mary stayed at home. Martha said to Jesus, 'Lord, if you had been here, my brother would not have died. But even now I know that God will give you whatever you ask of him.' Jesus said to her, 'Your brother will rise again.' Martha said to him, 'I know that he will rise again in the resurrection on the last day.' Jesus said to her, 'I am the resurrection and the life. Those who believe in me, even though they die, will live, and everyone who lives and believes in me will never die. Do you believe this?' She said to him, 'Yes, Lord, I believe that you are the Messiah, the Son of God, the one coming into the world...'

Then Jesus, again greatly disturbed, came to the tomb. It was a cave, and a stone was lying against it. Jesus said, 'Take away the stone.' Martha, the sister of the dead man, said to him, 'Lord, already there is a stench because he has been dead for four days.' Jesus said to her, 'Did I not tell you that if you believed, you would see the glory of God?' So they took away the stone. And Jesus looked upwards and said, 'Father, I thank you for having heard me. I knew that you always hear me, but I have said this for the sake of the crowd standing here, so that they may believe that you sent me.' When he had said this, he cried with a loud voice, 'Lazarus, come out!' The dead man came out, his hands and feet bound with strips of cloth, and his face wrapped in a cloth. Jesus said to them, 'Unbind him, and let him go.'

JOHN 11:17, 20–27, 38–44

I remember, when I was young, hearing a strange story come on the car radio. I have tried to track it down more recently, but it has proved elusive. It was a monologue, and the one speaking was Lazarus, back from the dead. It was powerful and a little disturbing, and it awakened a curiosity in me for this story I had heard, but clearly I did not comprehend as well as I had imagined.

How would it be, to be Lazarus?

What would he tell us?

But, we are racing ahead. Let us return to the gospel story. As we follow it through, it is worth being on the watch for the flowering of the themes sown in the prologue, at the very beginning, where John talks of light and life, the light that shines in the darkness and the darkness not overcoming it. We see in this story of Lazarus the beauty of that light and life breaking through, and also the power and depth of the darkness. If we are alert, we will also see the other great themes of the gospel: seeing the glory, grace and truth of God in the life of Jesus, and an invitation to belief. All these things open and flourish in the account of Lazarus, Martha and Mary.

So, after the healing of the man born blind – that breaking in of light into darkness – the conflict with the religious leaders is out in the open and they pick up stones in anger. Jesus withdraws, back to where his ministry began (10:40). It was here that John the Baptist had called him 'the lamb of God'. In this place by the Jordan, many believed in him.

Messages and prayers

While he is by the Jordan, a desperate message arrives saying that Lazarus, his beloved friend, is very sick. And he does not respond. For all of us who have prayed for healing for someone we love, or for the resolution of some terrible situation, we send our messages to God, and then, sometimes, nothing happens. This experience of silence is one all of us who have prayed encounter.

And yet, and yet, we pray.

I go through times when I find it hard to pray for a direct intervention, as in the healing of Lazarus. When I don't know how to pray, I ask God to accompany me, to be with me and to be with the one I am praying for. I find myself expanding my prayer – for others I know in similar circumstances, and then for those I don't know. I pray for the support that is there, or that it may be there. I ask if there are things I can do to be part of the solution. That is what, in practice, I do. Even when I don't know how to pray, or why I am praying, I find that I do.

And then there are times when we know prayers have been heard and answered. We can remember the joy of things falling into place, unlikely as it seems, of unexpected recovery, of things occurring at exactly the right time. It is good to remember these occasions; it helps us pray when we falter. It is good to continue to ask God for help in times of trouble. It is good to remember, too, that Jesus does respond to the message and come to Lazarus, in his time.

We have thought of the messages Martha and Mary sent as being like prayers. Maybe there is another way this part of the story teaches us about prayer. John does not tell us what Jesus was doing those two days he remains by the Jordan. When he finally arrives at his friend's graveside, though, he gives thanks that the Father has heard his prayers. So maybe what he is doing on the banks of that river, where God called him his beloved son, is praying.

There is certainly much for Jesus to wrestle with. If he goes to Bethany, he is going back to where his life is in danger. The act of going to Lazarus may cost him his life. Has the time come? Is he laying down his life for his friend? Is now the time to confront the last enemy, death?

The death and raising of Lazarus, this journey to the grave and into life, foreshadows the Easter story in all its brightness and strangeness. Also, in a very real and practical sense, the raising of Lazarus precipitates Jesus' arrest and all that follows.

So, while Jesus was waiting, was he coming to terms with what was going to happen and seeking the Father? John's gospel is very full of the bond between the Father and the Son.

> Prayer is nothing less than oneing the soul to God.
> Julian of Norwich[18]

Prayer also propels him into action, as it does now. It is not that he lingers by the Jordan because he does not care or knows that all will work out well at the end. We are not dealing here with a Saviour who is indifferent to the suffering of the world, but who is preparing to enter into it more fully than we can imagine.

He comes to the point of decision, of action.

When he says, 'Let us go to Judea again', the disciples are afraid. They know to go to Judea is to risk death. And, so, it proves to be. This road to abundant life, *zoe*, is a road that passes through darkness. Perhaps Jesus is wrestling with the way to life, the way through death.

There is work to be done.

Walk in the light

If they are going to go back to Judea, then they will need to walk, and ideally by day. Walking by night is a difficult business. Once again, Jesus says something simple and practical and relevant to the situation – if they are going to go, they had better go while it is light. We know, though, he has recently said, 'I am the light of the world', twice, and so the word 'light' stirs up thoughts of another kind of light. Life and light run through this gospel like shining threads. There is light here too, on the road to a friend's grave.

Jesus, the light, is going to wake him up.

Martha

Jesus arrives at Bethany to the news that Lazarus is four days dead and in the tomb – and to the greeting of Martha, who went out to meet him: 'Lord, if you had been here, my brother would not have died' (11:21).

Martha says more than this: 'But even now I know that God will give you whatever you ask of him' (11:22). Martha's confidence in Jesus seems to hold even in the face of his delays and her brother's death. We do not know what she expected might happen – maybe she didn't know herself, and was simply speaking in fresh raw grief. Perhaps she was throwing her whole self, her whole confidence and trust, on this dear friend who was unlike anyone else she knew.

> Jesus said to her, 'Your brother will rise again.' Martha said to him, 'I know that he will rise again in the resurrection on the last day.'
> JOHN 11:23–24

To Martha, this talk of rising may have sounded like a conventional consolation, and she takes it up, this hope, and places it on the last day, a day when the dead will rise. It is hope that death is not the end. It is a distant hope, though, for a distant future.

'I am the resurrection and the life.' In this one sentence Jesus moves that distant hope – a time, an event, a particular future thing – and says this instead: he is the resurrection, standing before her now. In him is life.

It is not a matter of doctrine and argument and intellectual assent. It is a deep, living truth embodied in the person of Jesus. Jesus is more than the one who rises from the dead on Easter Sunday, for others to look on and marvel, and believe if they can. He himself *is* resurrection, and that means something transformative for Lazarus, Martha and Mary, and all of us.

What might this mean? A great deal – an eternity's worth to discover! But maybe this is a place to start our exploration: to be caught up in Jesus, clothed and enfolded in his love and life, is to be living the resurrection life. Once again, this is the *zoe* – the Greek word used here and elsewhere most commonly translated 'eternal life'. When we say that, we tend to think about what happens when we die, if that is what we believe. But *zoe* carries the meaning of a quality of life, rich and full, abundant, that begins now. It is like the kingdom of heaven being close at hand, within you, very near, and it is spoken about in this way in the other gospels. This resurrection is a quality which Jesus holds now. This life is in him now. We can be part of that. Hildegard von Bingen, the twelfth-century composer, herbalist and mystic, wrote of *viriditas*, the greening life of the Holy Spirit, a sign of spiritual and mental health that flowed through creation.[19] She drew deeply on John's gospel and the idea of the living light.

Martha continues to hope for the life to come. That is a hope beyond death to hold on to – included in the loving dance of God, as we will explore later when we look at the vine. It is a dance, a life, which is not halted by death.

Love never ends, and nothing can separate us from the love of God (see 1 Corinthians 13:8; Romans 8:35).

'Yes Lord, I believe that you are the Messiah, the Son of God, the one coming into the world.' Martha does not immediately pick up on the point about the resurrection, but she does seem to grasp that it is all about Jesus – who he is. This is no moment for theology, for figuring things out – and fortunately that is not what is required. It is a moment of trust, of putting faith in Jesus, of leaning on her friend who she calls the Son of God.

The one coming into the world.

It is an interesting way of saying it. Maybe it carries the meaning of the emerging new life, a new way of being, dynamic and growing – something that continues to happen, perhaps for us too. Can we imagine what it might mean for Jesus to be the one who is coming into the world, even now?

After this powerful, raw conversation, Martha leaves to fetch her sister. I suspect Martha is watching over her sister's grief too. In times of grief, it helps not to be alone.

Mary

Mary didn't go out to Jesus when Martha did. Maybe she was overcome with sorrow. In difficult situations, it helps to remember that our responses do not follow the same script. We are who we are, perhaps more so when raw and exposed.

But, when Mary hears her sister saying to her that Jesus has come, she goes to him right away.

Jesus stays where he is. He has not yet come to the house. All things in their time.

Mary falls at his feet, weeping, surrounded by others who weep too.

She says the same thing as her sister: 'Lord, if you had been here, my brother would not have died.' She says no more than this. The tone, therefore, feels different. These are desperate, almost accusing words. Maybe they *are* accusing words.

The pain of the moment now is overwhelming. Jesus is described as being greatly disturbed, deeply moved, and he weeps. There is no talk here of denying the hope of the resurrection by grieving, no lack of faith in being overcome with emotion. Presumably, Jesus knew what he was about to do, and yet he enters fully into this grief. He may have held back from this moment precisely because he could see so clearly the depths of it.

What was it that moved Jesus? The loss of his friend, the pain of the ones who loved him and were left behind, are immediate causes. But maybe the whole weight of the world's death and grief – the stark reality of the enemy that is death, weighed on him too. The near reality, now, that death must be overcome by passing through it – by Jesus himself enduring it. The necessity. This is the way. This is what must be.

The way is hard, the way of life and light through darkness and death. The pain of death is very real – Jesus feels its reality, on his way to face it.

> He said, 'Where have you laid him?' They said to him, 'Lord, come and see.'
>
> JOHN 11:34

Jesus moves to stand by the grave with those who weep, and he weeps too.

Perhaps we can learn from this 'come and see' to invite Jesus into the darkest places in us. It is the same phrase Jesus uses to answer 'Where are you staying?' right at the beginning, inviting Andrew and another to follow him (1:35–39).

He will follow us too, even to the grave of one we love.

Life

So, they take Jesus to the cave tomb, with a stone across the entrance, and Jesus is again greatly disturbed. And, again, we wonder – how much did this feel like a vision of what was to come? The journey into the cave will be his. That darkness, those grave-clothes.

Jesus stands before the darkest place, crowded around with the grief of those who have lost one they love, and speaks resurrection over it. 'Take away the stone,' he says. Later, rolling the stone away will be the work of angels.

Martha, ever practical, has imagined the state her brother's body will be in by now. The stench of death and decay would be hideous. If the stone is rolled away, the contagion of death will be released among the living. Can she believe she will see the glory of God in such a place? Can we? This is no mountaintop experience. This is descending into Hades, as close as we can picture it.

The stone is rolled away anyway, and then Jesus prays a strange non-prayer. The prayer is for the sake of those listening, so that they and we may understand what is happening. He prays loudly before the open mouth of the cave, in the very jaws of death. He speaks to God of the prayers he has spoken, and we think of the two days, the long walk, the time open to God which seemed like delays and possibly even reluctance. We know he and the Father are one. We know he prayed about this moment. This raising, this resurrection, is so that they would know, we would know, that Jesus was from God.

> We have seen his glory, the glory as of a father's only son... No one has ever seen God. It is God the only Son... who has made him known.
>
> JOHN 1:14, 18

We see what God is like. God weeps at the grave of his friend, and then calls him out of that grave, back to life: 'Lazarus, come out!'

The text says that the dead man came out, bound with strips of cloth. What did John mean? The man who was dead? That we who watched were still thinking of him as a dead man? Jesus' next words feel momentous: 'Unbind him and let him go.' Lazarus was still bound in grave-clothes, his face covered, his hands and feet unable to move freely. He needed to be released from the trappings of death, as well as from death itself. We can be bound by many things, by fear, and debt, and illness, by the things that have been done to us, by unjust systems, by family history, by our cycles of addiction and self-destruction. Jesus sets the captives free and binds up the broken-hearted. Jesus binds us where we are falling apart, releases us where we are bound.

What was it like, at that moment, for Lazarus? What had happened to him? Where had he been? What was it like to feel the sun again, the air fill his lungs, to see his sisters, his friends and Jesus, who called him 'beloved friend', again? These are questions which so stirred my imagination as a child and stir it still.

Lazarus needed to be released from the grave-clothes, but maybe there were other kinds of letting go he needed now. People might crowd him, embrace him, long to touch him. When Mary Magdalene met Jesus in the garden, on that Sunday morning, Jesus said, 'Do not hold on to me' (20:17). I am reminded of that scene here. Perhaps there is a fragility, a mental and physical shock that needs time to adjust to this new way of being.

'Practise resurrection'

What would it mean to be a resurrection people – to participate with Jesus in making things new, to be part of the new heavens and new earth, to pray and work for his kingdom to come now, on earth, as it is in heaven? Is it possible to go deeper than believing in resurrection, to begin to practise it, to live as if it were the way things were meant to be? In any experience of darkness, perhaps we can take the courage from this story to enter into it, to not be afraid, to know there is a way out the other side. Even in darkness, we can look for signs of light.

The line 'Practise resurrection' from the poetry of Wendell Berry[20] has been taken as an inspiration by Shane Claibourne[21] and his companions in a project in Philadelphia, The Simple Way. A group of friends moved into the poorest part of the city and now seek to live the gospel of hope and resurrection where they are. They coach youngsters with their schoolwork and collect school supplies for them. They paint murals over ugly disused industrial buildings, and plant vegetables in land that no one is using. They take rubbish and make beautiful, useful things with it. In an area where it is easier to buy a gun than a lettuce, these things are good news. They partner with others to raise funds for college fees, medical fees, loans for new businesses; with builders to turn abandoned buildings into homes; with blacksmiths to beat guns into gardening forks. They seek to live as resurrection people in their neighbourhood, transforming it with hope and life, valuing people who feel abandoned by employers and politicians. They seek to set people free, to breathe new life, by living in the community, loving and serving all they encounter.

I find this model of being a resurrection people deeply inspiring. It is hope for the church, as well as for the world. The Simple Way is big on street parties, celebrations, festivals, joy. There are many groups of Christians around the world who seek to live out this abundant life in different ways. Many who see what is lost, forgotten, dead and abandoned as a place for the light of life to shine, for the resurrection power of God to transform. Resurrection is not simply a theological belief. It is a way of being, the new order of heaven breaking in to earth that flows from that belief.

Feast

One thing resurrection means, in this story of Lazarus, is an extravagant feast and an extravagant anointing (John 12:1–11).

The raising of Lazarus draws huge crowds. People saw Lazarus, and believed in Jesus. There is an interlude in the story (11:45–57) where we see that not all responded with joy. We see how the threat to Jesus grows. Caiaphas the high priest says that it is better that one man should die for the sake of the people. He knew this joyful, life-full outpouring of hope could pose a threat, could bring down the wrath of Rome. Later, of course, in AD70, a different sort of uprising did exactly that.

Now, this is a 'Jesus' uprising – of feasting, a celebration of an empty grave. The feast, the open house, is an image of the kingdom we have come across elsewhere in the gospels, in Jesus' parables of wedding feasts and banquets, of the hospitality of the Father's house.

As the feasting continues, Mary enters. In an extravagant act of thanksgiving, a prophetic act too, she pours out precious perfume and anoints Jesus' feet. She unbinds her hair, an undressing, a vulnerability, as she gives the most precious gift the house can offer – a jar of nard. This act of kneeling has its later echo: as Jesus kneels to wash his disciples' feet. I wonder whether Jesus was remembering this act of Mary's when he knelt before his friends.

Such abundance scandalises those present. Yet, Judas makes a valid point about the poor – it is consistent with Jesus' teaching, with the emphasis of the Hebrew scriptures. Some have used this exchange as a justification for neglecting the poor. I do not think this is valid. The disciples, having little as they did, were in the habit of giving to the poor, as is referenced more than once. One possible meaning of Bethany is 'house of the poor', so maybe the Lazarus family were involved in that work of care and hospitality.

When Jesus says the poor will always be with you, he is referring to Deuteronomy 15, where God promised a good, prosperous land, and that, if people live generously, justly and openly, there will be no poor. However, as people do not live like this, there will always be poor, and therefore, we must open our hands. The presence of poor people indicates the failure of the community to act in a way which removes poverty. It is a spur to economic justice and generosity.

If we are looking for a simple rule for the use of money, a clear instruction that will cover every eventuality, we will not find it here. Mary's gift is received; responsibility to those in need remains. Offering our best to God also means caring for those who have little (Matthew 25).

Mary's gift, an outpouring of extravagant love, Jesus took to be an anointing before his death. He experienced that love and generosity while he was still living and breathing. She had received her brother back from the dead, and she responded. 'From his fullness we have all received, grace upon grace' (John 1:16).

As Mary received, so she gave.

She kneels at your feet again,
pours out extravagant nard,
scandalous anointing of your warm, living feet,
unbinds her hair and lets it flow like water
over them, wiping them in such reckless
and tender thanksgiving.

Fragrance fills the room, the house, the night
as more people pour from Jerusalem to you,
to you, who comes to us in our weeping,
who shares our bread with us,
and brings us to such joy as this.[22]

Reflection and response

Study

Read John 11 and John 12:1–10.

John 11:4–6

- These are hard verses to read. Have you had experience of asking for help – in prayer or otherwise – and waiting for an answer? What was that like?

John 11:7–16

- The power of death seems very present in this whole section. What do you think it was like for the disciples, returning to Judea?
- What do you understand by Jesus' words about light? Is it something you can visualise in your own life?
- What about the image of death as a sleep? Can you think of examples of ways these words have influenced Christian writers and thinkers? Might the phrase help us understand how Jesus was seeing the death of Lazarus, or does it sound like a softening of a hard truth?

John 11:17–32

- We see differences in the way the two sisters responded to their loss. Why do you think that might have been? How does Jesus respond to them both?
- In this passage, we see individuals grieving as well as a community. Reflect on how much space, and how much support, we might all need to give and receive at difficult times. What has your experience been?

John 11:21–27

- Reflect on Martha's faith in this impossible situation, and on Jesus' words. What do you think Martha understood by them?
- What do you understand of this blurring of boundaries between life and death?

John 11:32–37

- Take some time to appreciate the depth of sadness expressed and experienced in these verses.

John 11:38–44

- Read this section slowly, several times. What words/phrases strike you? Is there anything in it that speaks into your current situation?
- Consider what Jesus says about God's glory, and about the grave-clothes. Do those words help you understand this miracle, and the role it plays in what is to come?
- In your own story, when can you recognise that Jesus was bringing resurrection, light and life? Has God been at work in your own times of shadow and darkness?
- How do you respond to Jesus' words on prayer? Have you had experience of prayers answered? What was that like?

Further study

- Follow themes through from the raising of Lazarus to Jesus' death and resurrection. For example, you could look at John 13:1–20, John 19:38–42, John 20:1–18.
- Look at Jesus' stories of the age to come that tell of banquets, wedding feasts, etc. Does any of this help us look back at the first sign recorded by John – the wedding at Cana in John 2:1–12? (See also Matthew 22.)
- You might also like to look at the book of Jonah (think about loss, forgiveness and resurrection); Psalm 130; 1 Corinthians 15 (Paul on resurrection); Deuteronomy 15. You might like to look at the story of the woman anointing Jesus from the other gospels (Luke 7:36–50; Matthew 26:6–13; Mark 14:3–9).

Isaiah 52:13—53:12

- Does this passage illuminate the coming suffering of Jesus for you? What particularly strikes you?

John 20—21

- Focus on the resurrection, and the difference it made to the disciples.

Revelation 21—22:7

- What do you make of these words about a new heaven and a new earth – the picture this paints of the destination?

Prayer and meditation

'Come and see' candle

Are there difficult things you are afraid to address in your thinking and memory? You might like to do this exercise with a trusted friend or counsellor. Invite Jesus to come with you, into your pain and loss. Imagine Jesus weeping with you. How does it go from here? You might finish by lighting a candle and giving thanks for Jesus' presence.

Music and art

Use one of the great requiems, such as Mozart's or Fauré's, to contemplate Lazarus' journey into the tomb and beyond. A shorter piece could be 'De Profundis' by Arvo Pärt (setting for Psalm 130). It is hard to think about death, even harder to face it for ourselves or those we love. Sometimes music, or a powerful story such as this, can help.

You could also use religious art of the crucifixion, a gospel narrative or the Isaiah passage above. You might like to consider a Stations of the Cross exercise, or an extract from a writer such as Julian of Norwich.[23]

Does it help to think that Jesus has gone before, and made a way?

Grave-clothes

Firstly, imagine yourself bound, as Lazarus was, with a cloth over your face. You might wish to use a strip of cloth around your hands and enact it. What does that feel like? What impact would it have?

Now, think of those things which may be 'grave-clothes' in your life: fear, debt, disappointment, selfishness, past experience or bad habits. Take your time and ask Jesus to release you from them.

Next, ask Jesus if there are any known to you who are bound in this way, and pray for them. Expand your prayer to your community and ask Jesus to set it free from its bindings. Ask if there are practical things you can do to set people free.

If you have used a strip of cloth, cut it and keep it as a bookmark to remind you of your freedom.

A prayer for when we are waiting

Use one of the waiting psalms as a prayer: Psalms 38, 40 or 62.

Creative response

Greening

You will need: a dry twig and a vase or jar, paper cut into leaves, green pencils or felt-tip pens, cotton.

Music suggestion: Hildegard von Bingen (perhaps 'Antiphon Caritas Habundant In Omnia').

Think of people and situations in need of new life – of healing and restoration and new beginnings. Write them down on the leaves, colouring them in with green. Ask for the Spirit of life to be given them. Tie them to the dry twig, giving thanks for new life.

Is there something you could do to support or cheer a sick person, or someone caring for a sick person? Or is there a seemingly dead situation that could be open to new life?

Life and service

Thanksgiving and generosity

Imagine Mary searching her home for something precious to offer. What do you have that you could give?

Make a list of resources and determine that every day you will give something – like a smile, a kind word, thanks. Think about things you could give each week for the next few weeks from your resources – and then do so.

What would extravagant generosity look like for you? Is there something you could do that draws close to that?

Give thanks for the life Jesus has given you.

At our toddler group, we marked Maundy Thursday with a blend of Jesus washing the disciples' feet and Mary's anointing. We offered the carers a foot-spa, and then massaged their feet with a fragrant lotion. We made posters with words and images from those gospel stories. Is there a situation in which you could do similarly?

Practise resurrection

Ask God whether there are ways you could 'practise resurrection'. God delights in using the flawed, the old and the cast aside, like Moses or Abraham. Remember how 'the one who was seated on the throne said, "I am making all things new!"' (Revelation 21:5). Ask Jesus to bring his resurrection life into yours now, to breathe into the dead and dark places. Similarly, ask him to do the same for those you love and for your community.

Ask, too, where you could be part of this process of making all things new, bringing new life.

Start simply – renew an old, thrown-away object: restore a piece of furniture, reuse old fabric for a sewing project, plant vegetables in a neglected place, make compost, use broken plates for mosaic, make something beautiful out of what has been cast aside.

Economic justice

Can you be more involved in economic justice? Some suggestions – fair trade, ethical banking, Christians Against Poverty, credit unions, cooperatives and transparent businesses, local and national politics.

Worship

If your usual worship practice is simple, seek out something more extravagant. If extravagant, try something simple. How did it feel? What did you learn?

Further reading

Shane Claiborne, *The Irresistible Revolution* (Zondervan, 2006)
Malcolm Guite, Stations of the Cross sonnets from *Sounding the Seasons* (Canterbury Press, 2012)
Julian of Norwich, *Revelations of Divine Love* (Penguin, 1998)
C.S. Lewis, *A Grief Observed* (Faber and Faber, 1961)
Tom Wright, *Simply Jesus* (SPCK, 2011)
Wm Paul Young, *The Shack* (Hodder, 2007)

Music

- Fauré, Mozart, etc. – the great requiems
- Gungor, 'Beautiful things'
- Hildegard von Bingen
- Arvo Pärt, 'De Profundis'

7

I am the way, the truth and the life

So, after receiving the piece of bread, he [Judas] immediately went out. And it was night.

When he had gone out, Jesus said, 'Now the Son of Man has been glorified, and God has been glorified in him. If God has been glorified in him, God will also glorify him in himself and will glorify him at once. Little children, I am with you only a little longer. You will look for me; and as I said to the Jews so now I say to you, "Where I am going, you cannot come." I give you a new commandment, that you love one another. Just as I have loved you, you also should love one another. By this everyone will know that you are my disciples, if you have love for one another.'

Simon Peter said to him, 'Lord, where are you going?' Jesus answered, 'Where I am going, you cannot follow me now; but you will follow afterwards.' Peter said to him, 'Lord, why can I not follow you now? I will lay down my life for you.' Jesus answered, 'Will you lay down your life for me? Very truly, I tell you, before the cock crows, you will have denied me three times.

'Do not let your hearts be troubled. Believe in God, believe also in me. In my Father's house there are many dwelling-places. If it were not so, would I have told you that I go to prepare a place for you? And if I go and prepare a place for you, I will come again and will take you to myself, so that where I am, there you may be also. And you know the way to the place where I am going.' Thomas said to him, 'Lord, we do not know where you are going. How can we know the way?' Jesus said to him, 'I am the way, and the truth, and the life.

No one comes to the Father except through me. If you know me, you will know my Father also. From now on you do know him and have seen him.'

Philip said to him, 'Lord, show us the Father, and we will be satisfied.' Jesus said to him, 'Have I been with you all this time, Philip, and you still do not know me? Whoever has seen me has seen the Father.'

JOHN 13:30—14:9

You do not know now what I am doing, but later, you will understand.

JOHN 13:7

Jesus knows that the time when he will be abandoned and betrayed by his friends, and then crucified, is getting close now. Knowing this, despite this, he loves them to the end (see John 13). Knowing that the Father had put all things into his hands, he strips and kneels and washes their feet. He gives them bread. In doing so, and by what he says, he tries to prepare his friends for what will come – must come. He does so with sadness and compassion. These are dark and difficult words. But, there is more. There is also a vision of love, service and life itself – the way of the Spirit, the Comforter. It offers them a way they can live when Jesus is no longer with them. They do not want to see ahead to such a time. This next 'I am' saying is part of all this preparation – showing them a way forward – a way that will endure. Jesus is that way. He will remain that way, even after.

We are not there yet, though. We need to stand back a little and see more clearly.

The towel

In John 13:1–20, Jesus gets up from the table, strips off his outer clothes, wraps a towel around his waist and kneels to wash his friends' feet. This is part of the way ahead – the way of love and service. It is an instruction for how they are to live when he is gone. They are to imitate this act – and a concrete task can help us through a difficult time. It is hard for them to receive it. This kneeling and washing, acting like a humble servant, is part of the self-emptying way that Jesus is following, a small foreshadowing of the self-emptying of the cross. The way of love and life passes through the darkness of death.

Jesus washes the feet of all of them, even Judas. He gives them all broken bread, even Judas. And then Judas steps out into the night, the darkest of shadows. Judas' motives may be equally dark, but one thing is clear – Jesus' love for him.

So Judas slips into the darkness, and what does Jesus say? That the Son of Man is now glorified. The word 'glory' is the root of five words in these sentences. Again and again, the word glory – full of light – shines out in this darkness. For the mood here is more sombre than earlier. If this were a symphony, the themes would be sounding in a minor key – darker, slower. Jesus' sadness is deepening. He wants his friends to understand, for to be alone in sadness is a terrible thing. Sadness and darkness are so much easier to bear when we have people with us who know what we are going through. And Jesus was indeed 'a man of sorrows, acquainted with grief' (Isaiah 53:3).

Glory

No wonder it was hard to grasp. This is what glory looks like: tying a towel around your waist (13:3–4), a friend leaving to betray you with the taste of bread still in his mouth (13:30), being lifted up on a cross. Such a long way from our idea of success. Such a long way from being exalted, praised or vindicated. This is the way to glory. This is the way of the kingdom. And Peter cannot follow now (13:36), but the time will come when he can, because of Jesus, going ahead. What might it mean for us, to know there is glory even here?

Then, Jesus again addresses his friends with compassion. He calls them 'little children' (13:33). He tells them plainly he will be with them only a little longer, that he is going to a place where they cannot come. But, again, he gives them something to do – something that continues the theme of washing feet. Their task, their commandment, is that they love each other: love each other in the way that Jesus loved them – washing their feet and, soon, laying down his life. This loving each other – loving even enemies, even one who would betray him – is the core, the crux quite literally, of both Jesus' life and teaching. It is the revolutionary way that will draw others. It is by the sign of love that his disciples will be known. It is the mark of an authentic Jesus-follower.

It is a tall order. I am aware of my own shortcomings in love, my own tepid or negligent response to the needs of others. Sometimes, very unloving actions flow from those who insist they are only following God's commands. It is worth remembering that the command Jesus gives is simply *to love*. It takes a major reorientation of our lives to build them around this command, to hold lightly other signs of belonging and to let love speak loudest in our lives. I wonder what it would be like if we did.

Where are you going?

Peter, though, has hardly heard these words about love. He is still thinking of Jesus leaving them. 'Lord, where are you going?' (13:36). He has not understood that Jesus means leaving them to die. Jesus is going; Peter wants to follow now but he cannot. It must have been heartbreaking to hear Jesus say he would deny him.

We tend to read 'Do not let your hearts be troubled' (14:1) as the beginning of a new thought. But we can read it as a response to the dismay that must have shown on Peter's face, and the faces of his friends, at this news of denying. Jesus knows that fear will get the better of Peter, that he will deny him before morning, but still seeks to reassure him. Jesus knows the reality of the darkness that will overcome his friend, but loves him anyway (see 12:46–50). Do not be troubled, the time will come to follow.

Our hearts are easily troubled. It is hard to trust for the right time. It is hard to trust that the trouble which burdens our hearts may be transformed. The disciples begin to see, and feel, the deep sadness of Jesus; they are coming to a deep, gut knowledge that something terrible is coming, even as Jesus seeks to reassure them.

He is not trying to reassure them by telling them that it's all going to be fine – not at all. He is giving them a frame, a way of seeing, an insight: what will happen must happen. He is putting it in a bigger and more necessary context. Something profoundly essential is happening – terrible as it is – that will ultimately work for the good. This is the only way.

A spacious home

Jesus gives them a picture of what the good will be – a picture of the host going on ahead to prepare rooms, or dwelling places. This is why he must leave, to unlock the door, to get things ready, to open and air the rooms. It is a large and spacious illustration, one that would conjure up Middle-Eastern principles of hospitality and welcome to all travellers that were foundational to their society but are uncommon in ours.

This picture of hospitality reminds me of the sheepfold Jesus spoke of a little while before, when he called himself the good shepherd.

> I have other sheep that do not belong to this fold, I must bring them also, and they will listen to my voice. So there will be one flock, one shepherd. For this reason the Father loves me, because I lay down my life in order to take it up again.
>
> JOHN 10:16–17

There is an expansion in these pictures, and a deep sense that Jesus will go to considerable pains, even to the loss of his life, to bring home the sheep, to make a place in the Father's house. Images of hospitality abound in the other three gospels for the kingdom – images of banquets and wedding feasts and wide tables. Here, we find these: a large and hospitable house, a generous sheepfold.

It is entirely understandable that Thomas replies, 'We don't know where you are going, so how can we know the way?' Now is the 'I am' moment: 'I am the way, the truth, and the life' (14:6). Can we think of a person as a destination? For that is what we are invited to do. Can we see being in the presence of Jesus as a way of being way, truth and life? The disciples are given a glimpse into this great meaning, a glimmer of glory in the night.

As we seek to walk the way of love and service, we walk along with Jesus. We remember that the earliest name given to Jesus' people was not Christians, but followers of the Way. We walk with Jesus, and with each other, on this path. That is the way.

Covered with the dust[24]

This was what it meant to be the follower, a disciple, of a rabbi: to follow, literally to walk behind, to share life with, to watch and in time to do the same. The disciple would be covered in the dust from his rabbi's feet because he stayed so close.

Perhaps it's time to rediscover the idea of the Christian faith as a Way. The resurgence of pilgrimage as a practice, the popularity of walking a labyrinth, are part of a hunger for more active expressions of faith. It has never gone away, though. John Bunyan's ever-popular *Pilgrim's Progress* shows us in dream-form the journey of a person through the world, falling into danger, learning wisdom on the way as he seeks to live out faith, growing as he goes. Each generation brings a renewed impetus to walk the walk, as well as talk the talk.

It is about transformation, not simply destination. We become as we go. We are seeking to live walking along the way with Jesus, drawing closer to the Father.

It keeps us as students, always looking to the master, not thinking we have all the answers, but knowing the one whose words give life. It saves us from the dangers of a closed mind. A position of humility is essential, both to love and to serve in the way Jesus did, and to be a disciple, a student.

It may mean going along unfamiliar paths. It may mean stepping away from safety and familiarity. The Bible narrative is full of journeys, of stepping out into the unknown, of stepping into an unknown future. Abraham and Sarah, the whole nation of Israel in the exodus, and many individuals, go. It is, it seems, in the going that they encounter God.

So, this knowledge that we are on a Way, an active, moving, dynamic thing, can be a call to be more courageous, more open to the possibility of God working outside our norms and expected static patterns. The Way is a person, the person of Jesus, and our security and confidence comes from knowing that we walk with Jesus and, although we do not fully know where we are going, maybe we do not need to.

Philip's request, 'Lord, show us the Father', is given the answer: 'Whoever has seen me has seen the Father' (14:8–9).

To be with Jesus is to see the Father. The way (being with Jesus) is also the destination (being with the Father). We have this picture of the Father's house after a long journey. It is an image worth dwelling on.

> All the way to heaven is heaven because Jesus said, 'I am the Way.'
>
> Catherine of Siena (1347–80)[25]

Home

It is an image of safety, of security, of hospitality, of community. Maybe these can be hallmarks of the way home, as well as of the home we are going to. We can live out this hope, this way of peace and love. We can cooperate with God in what God is already doing to spread this kingdom, as we pray for the kingdom to come. The way and the destination have much in common.

But not all. Not all. For there is a reason the disciples cannot follow Jesus yet. The way is being made, and the way is through the cross. It is too hard for his friends now, Jesus needs to go down into the depths of the grave in order to defeat death, to take the worst humanity can do and forgive it, and then rise again. By this Jesus makes the way, is the way and the gate: 'Through him God was pleased to reconcile to himself all things, whether on earth or in heaven, by making peace through the blood of his cross' (Colossians 1:20).

For Peter, the way involves the pain of denial, and the courage to accept the new beginning Jesus offers. But, even so, we are told not to let our hearts be troubled. Know that there is a purpose to what will happen. Jesus goes ahead and will come back to take us to where he is going. This is why we are not to be troubled – not because everything will work out fine, but because of the presence of Jesus, because the Father has a place for us.

Can we keep going, putting one foot in front of the other, knowing that we are not alone; keeping in step with the great flow of love and life that is the presence of the Spirit with us? Sometimes. And when we cannot, we can remember the compassion of this conversation, Jesus' tenderness with his distressed and bewildered friends. He knows they cannot understand now, but they will, later.

What is truth?

In a little while (18:38), Pilate will ask the above question. Truth seems a slippery concept in his hands, and he doesn't even wait for an answer. We live in an age when the Pilates of this world manufacture industrial-strength webs of words which so easily twist our thinking. It seems a timely question for us, lost in a sea of information and misinformation, not knowing what to believe.

There are whole schools of philosophy exploring epistemology – how we know what we know and how we justify our beliefs about the world. Religions spend much time exploring these issues. Important as they are, we will keep our focus here on Jesus – on what he might have meant, and what that might mean for us in practice as we live our lives.

What can it mean, though, that Jesus is truth? It is deep and many layered, but a few things are clear. It must tell us something about the kind of truth he means. Some languages, such as French, make a distinction between knowing something and knowing someone – *savoir* and *connaitre*. If we are to know the truth that Jesus is talking about here, we need to think in terms of *connaitre*. Knowing a person. Knowing their character, their preoccupations and priorities, something of their history, how they respond to situations. Truth is bound up with a person.

> You search the scriptures because you think that in them you have eternal life; and it is they that testify on my behalf. Yet you refuse to come to me to have life.
>
> JOHN 5:39–40

Jesus says this to the religious leaders who question him for healing on the sabbath. Once again, this is knowing a person rather than knowing a body of knowledge – even the scriptures. The disciples could literally follow the person of Jesus, know the person of Jesus. For us, it's not so clear. How do we find such truth?

We can read the gospel accounts – humbly, aware that we bring our own perspectives and preconceived ideas, but nonetheless reading for ourselves. We can ask the Spirit to lead us in all truth – which seems to require some walking. We can read the various books of the Bible and find an overarching story of love and redemption and goodness there. We can find there too the illumination of the Spirit, nudging hearts towards the God of love. When Jesus talks of leaving, and the Spirit coming, he talks of the Spirit of truth abiding with us, teaching and reminding us of all that Jesus has said (John 14:17, 26).

The Spirit also works through our own experience – practical knowledge of spiritual things – and can be a vivid guide. I have found that the study of the natural world – through science, through observation – helps me grasp more of the wisdom of the Maker, the *logos* behind all things. Traditions can also teach us much. We can pay careful attention to the experience of those who have gone before us, who have thought deeply, and entered deeply into the presence of God.

Attractive as absolute certainty is, I do not believe it is what we have been given. While we are sure we have the truth, we will tend to close our minds to thoughts that have not crossed our path before. We may become deaf to the leadings of the Spirit, even when God is nudging us to move deeper and fuller.

Thomas is good at questions – he seeks out answers. I am so grateful for the model of Thomas in John's gospel (20:24–29), with his honest determination to ask hard questions and find truth. Jesus respects and responds to such questions. It is good to dig deep, to search for truth, to go through doubt and question and difficulty without fear, if that is where the road is taking you.

I do not believe we should be afraid of truth where we find it. If God made all, if the earth and everything in it is the Lord's, and all people bear the image and likeness of God, we should expect traits of God to appear, to flash like light from unexpected sources.

Of course, we will disagree. We will see things differently. But we can find riches in our different perspectives. We can learn the disciplined work of listening to understand rather than to contradict. We can focus above all on loving and following Jesus, and loving and serving others. When we do that, the differences and disagreements slip into the background, become less important, cease to prevent us from loving God and loving each other.

The reality behind it all, the reality we can trust, is love. That is why Jesus goes on ahead through what we cannot, and then comes back for us again.

The way of love is not soft, comfortable or secure. It will take Jesus to hell and back. It will take him to the very worst that can be done to a human being. This is the way that humanity will see God's outstretched arms, and be liberated to enter abundant, overflowing life. Jesus is making the way.

Way, truth and life are here.

> In him was life, and the life was the light of all people.
> JOHN 1:4

Reflection and response

Study

John 13:1

- What do you know about the Passover? Do you see connections between Passover and the events that are to come? Do you see differences?
- Notice how love is mentioned as the driving force right at the beginning of the account. Go through the chapter making note of all the references to love. What do you notice?

John 13:2

- What do you make of the role of Judas in this story? How do you respond to Jesus including him in the foot-washing, and the breaking and sharing of bread?
- Have you experienced betrayal? What was that like? Have you ever let down a friend? Did anything help put things right?

John 13:3–20

- This is an extraordinary, momentous story. What does it tell us about the mission of Jesus and his character?
- How would you have reacted to Jesus kneeling before you? It seems that only Peter spoke – what might the others have been thinking and feeling?
- Look at the exchange between Jesus and Peter – how do we trust when we don't understand? How can we wait for 'later'?
- What do you understand by Jesus' words about being clean?
- What does this passage teach us about being a teacher or a leader? Can you think of examples where you have been served by a leader, or not? Are there ways you can reframe any leadership roles you may have towards love and service? What could you do?

John 13:21–31

- Some traditions speak of John reclining against Jesus, and hearing his heartbeat. What would that have been like?

- How would it have been to share a meal together with such undercurrents of suspicion and fear?
- What do you think of the contrast between Judas stepping into the night, and glory?

John 13:31–38

- Why does Jesus say to love one another is a new commandment? How do you respond to a command to love?
- What must it have been like for Peter to have his bold assertion undercut in this way?
- Have you ever trusted in God, even when your heart is troubled?
- What images come to mind when you think of 'my Father's house'?
- Have you tried to follow Jesus' way? What has that been like?

Further study

Exodus 12:1–28

- Consider more deeply these themes of the Passover: slavery and servanthood; a meal overshadowed by death and departing. Do these help your reading of the last supper?

Matthew 22:1–14

- The kingdom as wedding banquet. How does this story compare with the many-roomed mansion in John?

Ephesians 2:11–22

- How do you respond to the cross as a work of reconciliation? Do you think of it in terms of reconciliation to God, and/or to others?
- Hold the image of the people of God as a building in your mind, with Jesus Christ as the cornerstone. Is that like the image of the Father's spacious dwelling? What strikes you?

Philippians 2

- As you read this passage, think of Jesus kneeling before his friends. Does this passage help us understand the way to the cross? What does it mean to have the same mind and the same love?

Isaiah 52:13—53:9

- Jesus – a man of sorrows, acquainted with grief. Can this knowledge of Jesus' sharing the sorrow of humanity help? Has it helped you?

John 14:15–31

- How do you see the interplay of love, Spirit and command in this passage?
- 'I will not leave you orphaned; I am coming to you' (v. 18). What does this mean to you?

Prayer and meditation

Prayer for others

Fill a bowl with water. Cut out some flower shapes or small squares of paper. On one side, write the names of people you wish to pray for – for their life and flourishing. You may wish to focus on people you lead or influence. Colour the side you have written on in pencil or wax crayon. Fold the corners of the paper over, and drop them in the water, blank side down. Pray and watch the paper unfold.

Seeking God

> Love of the truth drives us from the world to God in prayer. The truth of love, which we discover there, sends us back from God to the world.
>
> William of Thierry[26]

> Whoever has seen me has seen the Father.
>
> JOHN 14:9

Begin your prayer seeking God. What does it mean for you that Jesus makes God known? What does that tell you about God? What has struck you in this chapter's passages? Maybe the foot washing, the new command, the Father's house. Ask God to help you go deeper, to understand what it means for you.

Is your heart troubled? Bring that to God, too (see specific exercise below). Listen for God's heartbeat of love.

Offer thanks.

Ask God to help you live out of love today.

Creative response

Foot washing

You will need: water, washable pens, paper, kitchen paper.

Imagine Jesus kneeling before you to wash your feet. Imagine you are there, in that upper room. What do you feel at first? What do you feel at the end? You might like to paint your response.

You could use washable pens on your hands, remembering things that do not fit with the command to love. Then dip your hands in water and watch them become clean.

Thank Jesus for his loving sacrifice and his example. Thank him for the gift of forgiveness.

Remember a time when someone offered you love, and practical service. What was that like? Remember a time when you did the same for someone else.

Think of what it means to be a leader like this. Where do you have opportunities to lay aside status and simply serve?

Seeing Jesus, seeing the Father

How do you see God? What do you see in Jesus in this passage? Does that alter, deepen, refresh your seeing of God? Take a piece of paper – write or draw/doodle words images from the life of Jesus, to help you see what God is like. Draw the 'I am's, and other words and actions that have spoken to you.

Hospitality of the Father

Time in the natural world can feel like receiving the kindly hospitality of the Father. I find Wendell Berry's poem 'The peace of wild things'[27] helps. It is a gentle bivouac along the Way.

Another poem I meditate on thinking of these words is George Herbert's 'Love (III)'.[28] You could begin by allowing your mind to be filled by one of these poems, perhaps memorising it, or a line or two.

Imagine and create. Have you experienced the hospitality of the Father? Can you imagine this many-roomed house? Draw, paint or write it out, and keep it as a reminder when your heart is troubled.

Troubled hearts

Bringing your heart before God, read through the John 14 passage. Let it speak, write out any words that strike you, and use them as the basis for your own written or drawn response. Use colours. What do you notice?

Imagine yourself, like John, reclining, listening to the heartbeat of Jesus. What does this do for you?

Labyrinth

Make a labyrinth. It could be a large one in the garden, temporary and marked with twigs or stones, on a roll of paper or old sheet for indoors, or a small one on paper you could 'walk' with your finger. Walk it prayerfully, becoming aware of the presence of Jesus with you as you make your way. You might like to research labyrinths before doing this, for example **labyrinth.org.uk** and **lostinwonder.org.uk**.

Life and service

Love

In every situation today, take this as your starting point: how can I best love and serve this person, these people?

My Father's house

Think about times you have received hospitality, and given it. What stays in your mind?

Can you expand your current practices of hospitality – even a small step? Circumstances and temperament vary, but there is always a small step.

How can we find a place for all? Ask the Spirit to guide you as you go through your day, that you may recognise the stranger, the angel, in those you meet.

Prayer walking

This exercise is adapted from *Supernatural Communication* by Rachel Hickson.[29] Pray for truth and life as you walk your everyday routes. Alternatively, you might use local maps and newspapers to pray for your area. As you walk, be mindful of Jesus, the Way, with you. Be thankful, and worship. Ask him what he sees and listen for answers. Be attentive.

Jesus spoke the words of John 14 at a distressing time, so pray as you walk for those in distress, that they may be comforted. Pray peace and blessing on homes you pass. Pray for truth and life.

Pray too for businesses, for dark alleyways, for green places, for roads and railways. Pray truth and life for all the ways you pass down.

Try to develop a habit of using your travelling time to be open to God, to what is going on around you, and to pray.

Pilgrimage

You may wish to go on a journey with a spiritual purpose and a particular destination in mind. You could travel far or go on a walking tour of local places of worship and ancient holy sites. You could use maps and photos to imagine yourself on such a journey if mobility is an issue. You can go with friends, or alone.

It helps to leave behind as much of your daily life as possible, and be as close as you can to the places you pass through and the people you see. So go on foot, or by bike, for as much as you can manage. Pray as you go. Expect God to speak to you as you go. When you reach your destination, spend time in quiet, being open, receiving.

Seeing God through Jesus

Consider the ways Jesus talks about being known, or making God known, in this section. How can we love each other, and follow Jesus, in such a way that people can glimpse God?

Can we live out being the image of God by becoming more like Jesus? What does it mean to love one another, and so make Jesus known?

Take some time to think this through. Write down your ideas. Then do one thing this week, and one thing the next, and so on.

Service and leadership

Consider ways in which you are involved in some form of influence or leadership. Think of ways in which you are demonstrating love and service, and ways in which you are not. Resolve to take some very concrete, practical steps to increase the love and service you offer.

Walking church

The Church of England Fresh Expressions movement includes some walking churches – more than just a Christian walking group. There are elements of prayer, the word, liturgy, hospitality, reflections, sometimes singing, that happen in the context of a walk. You can find out more by searching online for 'walking church' or 'forest church'.

A small group might wish to try out a version of the idea, or form a 'fellowship of boots', and see what develops.

Truth

Be on the lookout this week for where and how you learn about the world. Look at your news sources. Consider how you listen to more personal news from friends and colleagues. Whom do you trust and believe? If you do not already do so, consider fact-checking, and reading and viewing things from perspectives that differ from your own. What do you find out? Be particularly alert to this question: does this presentation of the facts encourage love and peace between people, or fear, hatred and hostility? Does it help or hinder me in loving God and loving others?

Further reading

Rob Bell, *Velvet Elvis* (Zondervan, 2005)
Rachel Hickson, *Supernatural Communication* (New Wine Press, 2006)
Brian D. McLaren, *We Make the Road by Walking* (Jericho Books, 2014)
John Ortberg, *If You Want to Walk on Water, You've Got to Get Out of the Boat* (Zondervan, 2001)
Andrea Skevington, *The Pilgrim Spirit* (Lion Hudson, 2007)
Desmond Tutu, *No Future Without Forgiveness* (Rider, 1999)
W.H. Vanstone, *The Stature of Waiting* (Morehouse, 1982)
Rowan Williams, *Being Disciples* (William B. Eerdmans, 2016)
Rowan Williams, *Tokens of Trust* (Canterbury Press, 2007)
Tom Wright, *The Day the Revolution Began* (HarperOne, 2016)

Music

- Ola Gjeilo, 'Ubi Caritas'
- Gungor, 'Beautiful things'

8

I am the true vine

'I am the true vine, and my Father is the vine-grower. He removes every branch in me that bears no fruit. Every branch that bears fruit he prunes to make it bear more fruit. You have already been cleansed by the word that I have spoken to you. Abide in me as I abide in you. Just as the branch cannot bear fruit by itself unless it abides in the vine, neither can you unless you abide in me. I am the vine, you are the branches. Those who abide in me and I in them bear much fruit, because apart from me you can do nothing. Whoever does not abide in me is thrown away like a branch and withers; such branches are gathered, thrown into the fire, and burned. If you abide in me, and my words abide in you, ask for whatever you wish, and it will be done for you. My Father is glorified by this, that you bear much fruit and become my disciples. As the Father has loved me, so I have loved you; abide in my love. If you keep my commandments, you will abide in my love, just as I have kept my Father's commandments and abide in his love. I have said these things to you so that my joy may be in you, and that your joy may be complete.

'This is my commandment, that you love one another as I have loved you. No one has greater love than this, to lay down one's life for one's friends. You are my friends if you do what I command you. I do not call you servants any longer, because the servant does not know what the master is doing; but I have called you friends, because I have made known to you everything that I have heard from my Father. You did not choose me but I chose you. And I appointed you to go and bear fruit, fruit that will last, so that the Father will give

you whatever you ask him in my name. I am giving you these commands so that you may love one another.'

JOHN 15:1–17

There is a way of seeing the overarching narrative of the Bible that looks like this: three gardens – the garden of Eden in Genesis, the garden tomb of the resurrection and the garden city of Revelation. If we hold this narrative in our minds, we see a story of flourishing, of hope, of new growth despite the winters we encounter. Gardens and their gardeners are a theme that runs through the whole Bible text. Gardens are both beautiful and necessary, a sign of a settled life, a sign of peace and security, a promise of plenty. And within the garden, the vine winds and trails its way through scripture, a sign of the people of God in both testaments, their frailty and fruitfulness, their need of a gardener to bring out their best flourishing, their provision of fruit and, more especially, wine to gladden the heart, wine soon to be poured out.

Mary, the first to meet the risen Jesus, mistakes him for a gardener (John 20:11–18). Gardener, as well as shepherd, seems to be a holy occupation.

The vine

'Rise, let us be on our way' (14:31). It seems that this story of the vine is told while walking, having left the upper room. It is likely, therefore, that Jesus was still thinking on the same dark themes as before, but that the fresh air, the movement, the sights around him caught his imagination. He brings forth this beautiful picture, giving another way of seeing to his friends who cannot yet understand. Such an image can remain in their minds and unfold its meaning slowly, bearing fruit at the right time. It can do that in our minds, too.

So, what were they finding so hard to understand? It was the huge and terrible necessity for Jesus' death. The Comforter, the Spirit, would come, but only after Jesus leaves them. It was beyond them to think that Jesus' death was necessary for something great to be accomplished. In the conversations surrounding this story of the vine, Jesus also speaks of that flow of love and life that includes Jesus himself, the Father, the Comforter and his followers – that is, us. These are the two great themes of the last words he spoke to his friends – his death, and the life that will come after – and they are entwined like the tendrils of a vine. It was a whole new way of thinking about life, and death too, and it is no surprise that it was incomprehensible to them.

Trinity

Even after all this time, it is hard enough for us to understand what Jesus meant. Yet, even so, it seems that the idea and experience of the Trinity, this mutual, loving, flow, is something we are now beginning to understand afresh. The flow of the internet, of interconnection, our greater understanding of the world in terms of systems such as climate science and chaos theory, new ways of interpreting cosmology and quantum mechanics all point to energy, flow, interconnectedness. This new understanding, coupled with a growing awareness of the perils of isolation, are changing the way we think of things. The Enlightenment's notions of sealed, self-contained individuality are breaking down; we are seeing passages like this in a fresh light and are perhaps beginning to understand anew in our generation. To do so, many of us are finding depth and rootedness in older traditions.

Rublev's (b. 1360s) icon gives us a picture of the Trinity, of God in community gathered around a table, gathered around, perhaps, a chalice of wine. Each of the three figures bows their head slightly to the other, each gaze holds the gaze of another. As we have explored John's gospel together, we have seen that John shows us a loving community at the heart of all things: God who models community. In a little while, close to the end, Jesus will pray that we will be one –

more than that – may be drawn into this community, may be part of this fellowship of love, to gather even around the table (John 17). Maybe there is room for us.

Art historians have uncovered something surprising about the icon. There is a space at the table, down at the front, where traces of glue have been found. It is believed that once there was a mirror here, so that the person gazing at the icon would see themselves seated at the table, invited and drawn into the loving flow of God.[30]

We do not need to be perfect before we are loved and welcomed. It is in this love that we are made perfect.

As we read this song of the vine, we will consider it in the light of this understanding of the Trinity as movement, as dance, as mutual life and love. This is *perichoresis*,[31] the movement at the heart of God described by John of Damascus (d. 749) among others. We read, alert to the flow of the Spirit in the vine. Interpreters over the last couple of centuries, when individualism was the cultural norm, have tended to assume it was easy to identify an individual branch as an individual Christian, separately plugged in, or not plugged in, to the vine. Gardeners will know that plants do not divide up so easily; the stem and branches flow together and branches multiply into others. I do not think Jesus was intending us to think about the vine in terms of its separateness, its divisibility, but rather this unity of love and life and flow of Spirit.

Herod's vine and the vine of Israel

Let us return to Jesus, walking with his friends through the night. It is possible they were walking within sight of the temple, on the hill at the heart of Jerusalem. So, as well as the growing vines fragrant about them, perhaps Jesus was drawing attention to the great golden vine that Herod had installed over the door to the sanctuary.

> The gate opening into the building was, as I say, completely overlaid with gold, as was the whole wall around it. It had, moreover, above it those golden vines, from which depended grape-clusters as tall as a man.[32]

Herod had lifted it up, a giant vine, like the huge bunches of grapes the spies reported when they said the land could not be taken (Numbers 13:17–24). That story represented the plenty of the good land they would be entering. Who would go hungry, who could be sad, in a land of such vines? This golden vine reminded the people of their identity – but, also, subtly changed that identity. This vine seems to have forgotten that it is fruit for a humble people. It is golden, like a symbol of empire, like something from Egypt or Babylon, like an idol even. It represents a national identity that celebrates the wealth and power of a local, petty tyrant, and also comes to pose a threat to the empire of Rome. Rome wants its conquered states less confident, weaker.

It also served a practical and beautiful purpose. This vine was where thank-offerings were hung – branches and flowers and fruit and grain. It was decked with natural beauty, the fruit of the land, the thanks of the people. As such, it was a precious thing.

It would have reminded the people of those garden images, those vine images, that recur again and again in the Hebrew scriptures. We will look at one of them – from Isaiah 5:1–7. The song begins:

> Let me sing for my beloved
> my love-song concerning his vineyard:
> My beloved had a vineyard
> on a very fertile hill.

It is full of beautiful longing, of broken-hearted disappointment. It is a compressed tragedy, a tale of how the nation will come to be destroyed. For all the love and care that God the gardener lavishes on this vineyard, it does not yield good grapes, but wild or bad ones. Then, from verse 5 onwards, comes the description of what will happen to the land – the hedge and wall will be taken down, and it will be devoured and trampled. Many scholars believe this refers to the further wave of invasions that will occur, by Babylon, and that the scribes who collated the scriptures during the time of the exile in Babylon would have seen words such as these as speaking particularly to their situation.

As I read this song, I wonder if those who had lived through or heard of the Roman destruction – like John's first readers and hearers – might see an echo of Isaiah's song of the vineyard in Jesus' words. Maybe they also refer, in part, to what will happen to the nation as Rome sweeps in. The revolutionary way of love, rather than swords, is the Jesus way – a different kind of kingdom, with a very different king. Like a low, trailing vine.

Reading Jesus' words about the vine after the Isaiah passage, we see that his song of the vine is more tender, compassionate and hope-filled than Isaiah's prophesy. His vine-grower tends the vine; he does not break down its protection.

The true vine: Jesus

As Jesus and his friends walked in the dark past vineyards, the image of the vine was real, fragrant, touchable. This song was no distant allegory. It was before them. What would they have glimpsed, in the thin light?

A winter vineyard looks as dead as dead can be. The bark flakes and pulls away. But, here, in the spring, buds would have been bursting out. What appeared dead was returning to life, throwing out tendrils, leaves, maybe blossoms. They knew the importance of the vine, and the care and wisdom needed to tend it and make it fruitful. Passover required the drinking of four cups of wine; each one had a significance, and they had drunk them with Jesus. Their blood was warmed with wine as they walked through the chill of night.

As Jesus walks, he begins: 'I am' – I am the vine. The Greek grammar is quite emphatic – *the* vine, the true vine, he says. It seems to me that he is aware of the contrast with those other vines – the image of Israel, later to be trampled, and Herod's ostentatious golden one.

And in the spring, sap runs through its veins like blood – it pours through, swelling the hidden buds. This is a kingdom vine. The way life flows through it is like the way the Spirit will sustain Jesus' followers after he has gone. The vine is loved and cared for by the Father. God alone is the gardener of this vine.

Remember how, in Genesis (2:8), God planted a garden, and gave humanity the job of caring for it: 'The Lord God took the man and put him in the garden of Eden to work it and take care of it' (2:15).

In this darkest evening, the evening of his betrayal, Jesus may be thinking back to this image of Eden. He may be remembering the stories of God's good intent. God is the gardener. We are to take care of the garden. The Hebrew word here is the same as the one used for the work of the priests in the tabernacle. Caring for the garden is sacred work.

Now, in this song of the vineyard, we are told that it is God's job to prune and clean, ours to remain. Pruning is skilled work. Prune at the wrong time, when the sap is rising, and the vine bleeds out. It is not our job. We do not know enough to judge which parts to remove, to clean.

We may think we know what this pruning is, but let's look again at John 15:2. Many translations say 'prunes' or 'cuts off'. The Greek word is *airo*, which can mean to lift up or take away. Ancient Middle-Eastern vines were trained close to the ground. It is possible that this verb means to lift up a trailing branch that has fallen to the ground. Bring it to the light, so it may bear fruit. This would be a powerful remodelling of the broken vineyard of Israel, with Jesus offering us a new vineyard based on love, mercy, compassion and forgiveness.

We should not be surprised, though, to find reference to cleaning or pruning. If we are honest about our lives, we see things that grieve us and others, things we might even be freed by losing. It is easy to overlook Jesus' teaching about the seed that must fall to the ground, about loss, about the blessings that belong to those who lack, who are waiting for the coming of the kingdom (Matthew 5). In the kingdom, our losses can be gains. The Franciscan tradition calls this path of loss the 'little way' and practises it joyfully, despite its poverty.

It is clear that the gardener's purpose is the flourishing of the vine; the picture is tender and nurturing. Life does not always feel like that. Jesus knows very terrible things are about to happen. He is giving his followers hope that in time, good things will come after and – in the case of his death – because of them.

And, although all this helps us understand the theology of loss, we must remember, in this song of the vineyard, that we do not prune – even ourselves. Our job is simply to remain.

Remain

To a group of people who will soon be scattered in the darkness, who will abandon him, Jesus talks of remaining, abiding. He talks to them, assuring them they are already connected to the vine, already clean. What will happen does not change that for them. He says this first, at the beginning of the song. All else that follows is held within the certainty that they are part of the vine.

Here is the melody of the song, and this is what we need to treasure – that we are also part of this vine, the sap flows through us.

The heart of it all is remaining in Jesus, as Jesus remains in the Father; remaining because of love, so that joy may be complete. We may not understand, but we can hold open the possibility of this love and grace and belonging.

> Here, I feel, is the secret: not asking how I am to get sap out of the Vine into myself, but remembering that Jesus is the Vine – the root, stem, branches, twigs, leaves, flowers, fruit all indeed... I have not got to make myself a branch. The Lord Jesus tells me I am a branch. I am part of him and I have just to believe it and act upon it.[33]

There is such security in this acknowledgement that we are already branches – we are part of the vine. Otherwise, it soon becomes another thing to worry about – another thing to do, another way we can fail and fall. We can be preoccupied with our own status, or lack of it, in the vine. Such preoccupation seems counter to the emphasis on love. How good to know we don't have to work out how to get the sap into us! It flows. That is the nature of the vine. It already is.

There are some 'ifs' – and it is hard to know how to read them. I believe Jesus means what he says when he says that we are fully connected, not separate in the vine. But we all know it doesn't always feel like that. For our joy to be complete, I think we must wake up to this deep truth that we are loved and included. We can choose to direct our gaze at the beauty of the vine and how good it is we get to be part of it, however we feel. Jesus is saying, again and again, that it's all about love: that the closeness of the love Jesus has with the Father is something that includes us too. The song of the vine is a song of love. And its outworking is a dance of love, between Jesus, the Father, the Spirit and us.

It is interesting to note the language John uses to describe God in his gospel. It is mainly the language of relationship. In particular, when Jesus talks about God, he speaks of Father. He speaks of himself as Son, and the Spirit he calls Counsellor or Advocate. He does not talk of God in terms of attributes – mighty, holy, everlasting – but as Father. Remaining seems to be an awareness that we are part of the vine and openness to this deep connection, knowing that we abide in love.

Alongside this dance of love and abiding, Jesus holds up the opposite, the contrast, the not abiding. He often speaks in this way, drawing on the Hebrew tradition of balancing opposites. Jesus was, I believe, speaking tenderly to his bewildered and grief-stricken friends, helping them make sense of the pain he and they were about to go through.

There is a warning about falling away, about those branches who are already cut off. It may be a foil to the talk of abiding, to show the power of abiding. It could mean other things too. Jesus could be thinking of Judas, with compassion and grief. It is also possible that Jesus, and John in his recording, was thinking of the fate of Jerusalem. John's early readers and hearers would know that over a million were killed, and the city was burned by the Romans. If that is so, it picks up on the earlier reading of the vine as the nation of Israel. However we read these verses, there is no doubt that the message Jesus wants us to hold on to is the message of remaining – remaining in love.

This picture of the vine is about remaining, even through cleaning and pruning. Above all, it is about allowing the work of the Spirit to flow through us, receiving and open to the love of God, letting it fill us and soak us, nourishing us that we may, in turn, nourish.

Fruit

We have talked about abiding, remaining, but the purpose of the vine is the fruit and the purpose of the pruning is to increase the vine's capacity to bear fruit. As Jesus continues his song of the vineyard, we see this fruit linked to a circular pattern of love – it begins with the Father for the Son, flows from the Son to humanity, who are then, for the second time, commanded to love in their (our) turn. The outcome of all this is joy – Jesus' joy will be in us and our joy will be complete.

Love, joy... from there, we are naturally drawn to another mention of fruit in the New Testament – the fruit of the Spirit.

> By contrast, the fruit of the Spirit is love, joy, peace, patience, kindness, generosity, faithfulness, gentleness and self-control. There is no law against such things.
>
> GALATIANS 5:22–23

The branches attached to the vine have the life of the Spirit flowing through them. There is beauty in a fruitful vine, with its leaves, blossom and, in time, the ripening fruit. Our lives, filled with the flow of the Spirit, can have such beauty. The life of Jesus, flowing through us, is transformative. Maybe Jesus is telling us here how the Spirit works, how our lives can be part of something greater. Connection to the source of all life and love leads to flourishing. We are not isolated, purposeless, lonely individuals. We are part of the something greater, and we can live out our lives fruitfully.

We must remember that this fruitfulness may not look anything like an easy life. The fruit is crushed to make wine. Jesus was very soon to die, and most who listened first to this song of the vine faced martyrdom. But we do know that such a collection of qualities as the fruit of the Spirit can lead to contentment, peace, joy and an outpouring of generosity and goodness.

Goodness, like all the fruit of the Spirit, grows slowly. It needs the warmth of the sun to ripen and sweeten it.

Whatever we may consider the fruit to be, Jesus quite clearly commands us to love each other, here for a second time. This is the heart of it – of abiding, of following. Everything else slips into the background in comparison. Jesus shows us that God seeks to extend the dance, to include all, and we can allow that love to flow through our veins so that we too can stretch out a hand, as Jesus does, to draw another into the great dance of love. It is the same love, flowing through us all. We participate in the flowing life, the love, the light of God, learning how to love and serve, learning how to hold on to God with one hand, while stretching out with the other. So, the vine grows.

Reflection and response

Study

As you think about the passage using the questions below, consider what Jesus may have been saying about community and flourishing.

John 14:25–31

- Jesus is no longer talking about going ahead, leaving, but about what will come next. At this point in their story, what does Jesus want the disciples to know about the Holy Spirit?
- Have you felt that the Holy Spirit is teaching you? In what ways?
- In this time of fear and confusion, Jesus says he is leaving peace for his followers. How can we enter into that peace?
- Jesus is emphasising the inevitability of what will happen, and it is hard for the disciples to understand. How would you put it in your own words?

John 15:1–4

- What do you think the image of the vineyard meant to the disciples?
- Consider also Psalm 80:14–16; Matthew 20:1–16; 21:33–43. Do any of these help our understanding?
- In verse 2, the Greek word *airo*, usually translated 'cuts off', also has the possible meaning of 'lifts up'. In this context, it could mean that a trailing, fruitless branch was lifted up into the sun. What do you think of these two meanings here?
- Have you experienced things in your life that you would describe as pruning? What was that like? What was the outcome?
- Read verse 4 again. We tend to think of ourselves as independent. What can we learn from the vine image? Are we dependent on each other, too?

John 15:5–8

- What is the purpose of the branches?
- What do you understand the fruit to be?

John 15:9–14

- Do these verses help us understand Jesus' meaning? Do they clarify what the fruit is?
- What do you think of the circular connection between love and obedience here?
- How do we obey the command to love in verse 12? What is it like if we do, and if we don't?

Further study

- Read the account of the wedding at Cana (John 2:1–12). Reflect on the symbolic meaning of the empty jars used for religious cleansing, here filled with fine wine at a wedding.
- Ephesians 2:1–22. Consider Christ's work in bringing unity to people who consider themselves divided, and in bringing near those who are far off. Work through this passage, with thanksgiving. Consider its implications for your life and community. Who seems far away to you?
- Colossians 1:15–20. How does this image of Christ connect with your thoughts on the vine? How do all things hold together in Christ?
- Ephesians 4:1–7; 1 Corinthians 12:12–27; John 17:20–24. Consider these passages that talk of unity, of the church, and which use the image of a body to describe it. What does that tell you about what Jesus desired for his followers? Are there ways you can work for peace and unity between believers where you are? If you are not in fellowship with other Christians, are there gentle ways you might be able to connect?
- 1 Corinthians 12:31—13:8. Jesus commands us to love one another. Take some time to consider what that means in the light of this passage. Think of one thing you can do this week to live in a more loving way.
- Passages for further reading: Isaiah 27:2–6; Jeremiah 2:21; Hosea 10:1–2; Ezekiel 15:1–5; 17:1–21; 19:10–15; Psalm 80.

Prayer and meditation

Lectio divina meditation – rooted and grounded in love

Read Ephesians 3:14–19, asking God to speak to you by drawing your attention to a word or phrase. Read the passage out loud, slowly, twice, leaving silence between and around the readings. See where your attention snags, what strikes you, and ponder that. If you are with others, hold a time of silence, then share your words or phrases.

Read again. On the last reading, be alert to anything that applies to you or your situation directly, any place where the Holy Spirit may be moving or guiding you. Thank God for what you have learned.

> As the Father has loved me, so have I loved you. Now remain in my love.
>
> JOHN 15:9 (NIV)

Celtic circling prayer

> Christ be with me, Christ within me,
> Christ behind me, Christ before me,
> Christ beside me, Christ to win me,
> Christ to comfort and restore me.
> Christ beneath me, Christ above me,
> Christ in quiet, Christ in danger,
> Christ in hearts of all that love me,
> Christ in mouth of friend and stranger.
>
> From St Patrick's Breastplate[34]

Celtic circling prayers such as this are usually in a natural walking rhythm. They are good to commit to memory, to take with you as you go through your day into any and all situations, to help keep you grounded in the love of Christ, and aware of his presence.

Open to the Spirit

At the beginning of the day, take a few minutes of silent prayer, opening yourself up to the flow of the Spirit. Keep bringing yourself back to this place during the course of the day. It might help to have a card in your pocket with 'I am the vine' written on it, or a picture of leaves and grapes. Hold in mind how 'remain' is connected to 'love' in the passage.

Liturgy of the vine

Use this liturgy with a group, inviting everyone to participate in the responses in bold.

Jesus, you are our true vine
Keep us rooted in your love
Jesus, you are the life that flows through us
Keep us open to you
Without you, we wither
Help us to understand your pruning
Without you, we cannot bear fruit
Help us to recognise your cleansing
We long to be fruitful for you
You command us to love one another
Give us strength and grace to love
The branches of the vine entwine and support each other
Help us know that we are one in you
In you is abundance of life
In you is the fruitfulness of the grain that falls to the ground
Bring forth fruit in our own lives
In you the grapes ripen in the autumn light
And the fields are white with harvest
Deepen your image in us
So our lives bear the fruit of your Spirit: love, joy, peace, patience, kindness, goodness, faithfulness, gentleness, self-control.
Amen

Creative response

Drawing meditation

Gather some drawing materials and paper. If you have grapes and/or vine leaves or prunings, lay them on the table. Read through John 15:1–17, perhaps out loud, and notice how the words 'love', 'remain' and 'fruit' are repeated. Each time you come to one of those words, pause for a moment and allow its meaning to unfurl like the leaves of a vine.

Now, draw a fruitful vine. You might like to draw in the style of Celtic knot patterns, with intricate and interconnected lines. As you draw, think about how you are connected to Jesus and draw life from Jesus, and think too of your brothers and sisters in Christ. Meditate on the love and the life that binds you together.

As you draw, imagine the sap flowing through the vine, bearing water from the rain and nourishment from the soil.

- Are there things you can do to draw more nourishment from the roots of this vine?
- Can Jesus become more fully the root of your life?
- Remember the three words: love, remain and fruit. Can you express them in your drawing?

As you draw freely, see what meaning and truth emerges.

- What is the fruit like on your vine?
- Are there things that need pruning for the vine to be more fruitful?
- How does the Father, the great gardener, tend this vine?
- Pray for patience and fruitfulness as God works through and in your life.

You might like to finish by eating (and sharing) grapes.

Life and service

Connection and community

Take some time to connect with people in your community. Be on the lookout today, this week, for ways you can build connection with those around you. It can be as simple as taking a few minutes to speak to a neighbour, smiling at a passer-by or something more. Loneliness and disconnection are major themes of our times, a source of much unhappiness. The first 'not good' recorded in Genesis is being alone.

Observe your community for a while; walk around looking and praying for eyes to see. Then list ways you might be part of making a stronger community. Ideas could include:

- using local shops, facilities, public transport
- walking or cycling where you can
- becoming involved in local groups, societies, politics, schools
- with others, noticing the needs in your community, and finding ways to bless and reach out – the elderly or housebound may require help, or young families, etc.
- litter-picking the streets around you, or clearing snow or leaves as appropriate
- supporting the work of credit unions or Christians Against Poverty
- volunteering
- investigating community pantries – 'Leave what you can, take what you need' – an open cupboard in a public place where people can donate and take food and other essential items
- making it a policy to greet those you see, those who serve you in shops, with a smile and a kind word; be open
- connecting with those in your neighbourhood around food or wine.

As you do any of these things, think of the power of connection, meditate on the Trinity, and know you are able to love and to bless those in your path.

Caring for the garden

Our first task, in Eden, was to care for a garden God had planted.

Here are some suggestions for what you might like to do: growing food, perhaps in waste land; community gardening projects; mental health gardening projects; gardening as meditation and connection with the earth.

Investigate seed and plant swaps in your area. Find ways to care for and bless the ground where you live. Cultivate those green shoots, those signs of hope.

Further reading

Brian McLaren, *The Great Spiritual Migration* (Convergent, 2016)
John Ortberg, *Soul Keeping* (Zondervan, 2014)
Richard Rohr, *Falling Upwards* (SPCK, 2011)
Richard Rohr, *The Divine Dance* (Whitaker House, 2016)

Music

- Something by Hildegard von Bingen, perhaps 'O noblissima viriditas', remembering her principle of life-light, of greening *viriditas*, which she saw in plants as well as people.

9

I am he

'Righteous Father, the world does not know you, but I know you; and these know that you have sent me. I made your name known to them, and I will make it known, so that the love with which you have loved me may be in them, and I in them.'

After Jesus had spoken these words, he went out with his disciples across the Kidron valley to a place where there was a garden, which he and his disciples entered. Now Judas, who betrayed him, also knew the place, because Jesus often met there with his disciples. So Judas brought a detachment of soldiers together with police from the chief priests and the Pharisees, and they came there with lanterns and torches and weapons. Then Jesus, knowing all that was to happen to him, came forward and asked them, 'For whom are you looking?' They answered, 'Jesus of Nazareth.' Jesus replied, 'I am he.' Judas, who betrayed him, was standing with them. When Jesus said to them, 'I am he', they stepped back and fell to the ground. Again he asked them, 'For whom are you looking?' And they said, 'Jesus of Nazareth.' Jesus answered, 'I told you that I am he. So if you are looking for me, let these men go.' This was to fulfil the word that he had spoken, 'I did not lose a single one of those whom you gave me.' Then Simon Peter, who had a sword, drew it, struck the high priest's slave, and cut off his right ear. The slave's name was Malchus. Jesus said to Peter, 'Put your sword back into its sheath. Am I not to drink the cup that the Father has given me?'

JOHN 17:25—18:11

This is the decisive moment, in 18:4, when everything changes: Jesus steps forward, moving away from his friends. He steps unarmed towards the guards, soldiers and Judas. This step delivers him into the hands of violent men. And yet, and yet.

In his very quietness, quiescence, there is power and strength they do not understand. For their power is no power. Jesus has freely chosen to drink from this cup of betrayal and suffering and death. He knows what is to come. He steps forward, into all that is to come, knowing this to be the way of justice, love and peace. He steps forward, knowing this is the way to something unimaginably great – overcoming and forgiving the worst evil humanity can do. But also, it is an immediate, personal, loving step – he keeps his friends safe, draws the eyes of the soldiers away from them as he enters their circle of glaring torchlight.

> 'For whom are you looking?'
>
> 'Jesus of Nazareth'
>
> 'I am' – *ego eimi* – 'I am he.'

In our reading of the gospel story, we can miss that this is a powerful 'I am' saying – we do not render it so in English. The soldiers and all who come to arrest him do not miss it. The words *ego eimi* – 'I am' – sound out three times in this passage. Jesus' layered identity is brought before us, and the soldiers, as the words 'Jesus of Nazareth' are immediately answered with 'I am'. Those who came to arrest Jesus are overwhelmed by these powerful words, and their more powerful meaning. They step back and fall to the ground. This is the great 'I am' of the burning bush in the shadowy brightness of the soldiers' torches. We are on holy ground.

Swords

Peter must put away his sword, and he does. Jesus undoes our common narratives of violence – killing, defeat of our enemies, power and control are not the way of the cross. Luke (22:51) records Jesus healing Malchus, the one Peter wounded. Even now, this is how Jesus loves his enemies.

There is a very moving 14th-century painting in the Chapel of the Holy Innocents at Norwich Cathedral which shows the arrest of Jesus. Jesus is at the centre, with soldiers around him. Judas is on his left, embracing him, and Jesus receives this embrace, moving slightly towards it. And Jesus' other hand rests on a poor naked scrap of humanity, Malchus, restoring his ear. It is all one beautiful, graceful movement. This movement, this gesture, seems to transform even the betrayal of a friend, turning it into something life-giving for the naked soldier. Even in all his ugliness, he is healed. At some point, someone has scratched away Judas' lips and eyes, presumably unable to bear the betrayal. But Jesus bore it; he submitted to it.

The path of the sword is not the way of the cross. For love and life to triumph over cruelty, separation and death, Jesus chose this way. It is the only way. He will receive betrayal and violence, and give back healing and forgiveness. The soldiers came at night, under cover of darkness, and this is how they were received. Jesus, unarmed, steps forward and meets them, graciously and powerfully. To come so with swords feels a cowardly act. Even with their swords, even under cover of darkness, they fall to the ground. This small drama is a foretaste of the meaning of what will be, on the cross. An apparent victory turns into defeat for all the darkness and death of the world, and all that leads to darkness and death. And all of it is greeted with forgiveness there, on the cross, all the worst that humanity can do.

I am not

Patterns of language are important in John, the most poetic of the four gospels. We will bear that in mind as we read on (18:15–27). Peter follows Jesus, and the soldiers who arrested him, to the courtyard of the High Priest. We notice that Peter, so close to that power, chills even as he stands by the fire. The energy that sustained him in the heat of the arrest has left him, and fear creeps in. He denies Jesus, as Jesus said he would. He denies him three times. The words Peter says are: 'I am not'.

Could this be the shadow of Jesus' 'I am'? Bishop Martin Seeley, in a Good Friday reflection, drew a connection between these sayings: Jesus' great 'I am' is countered by Peter's 'I am not'. Notice how John records Jesus' 'I am': he does so three times – Jesus says it twice, and John reports it again once. John forms a similar pattern with Peter's 'I am not's – Peter says it twice in direct speech, and John reports the third time. It is subtle, but the echo is strong. For on this dark night, Peter distances himself from Jesus.

I am not.

It bears a heavy load of meaning, this 'I am not'.

We may know how this story with Peter continues; how, after Jesus rises, he cooks Peter breakfast and instructs him to take care of the flock, to feed the lambs, three times, one for each denial. Forgiveness and renewed inclusion in the great flow of life and love and hope and nurturing are offered three times. Peter is restored (21:15–19).

I am

'I am' is such a common construction, something we say many times each day. It is also a very deep mystery. Who are we? How do we define ourselves? We have seen that, in the mouth of Jesus, it links those two great things – the everyday experience of bread and plants and light and life, and the deepest mystery of being, the 'I am' of God, who is beyond our comprehension, but who longs to be known in these very elements of life. In seeing Jesus, we see the nature of this God, and Jesus invites us to participate in this light and life with him.

> As you, Father, are in me and I am in you, may they also be in us, so that the world may believe that you have sent me. The glory that you have given me I have given them, so that they may be one, as we are one, I in them and you in me, that they may become completely one, so that the world may know that you have sent me and have loved them even as you have loved me.
>
> JOHN 17:21–23

Perhaps we too, in all our common, daily life, can connect these two things. Our lives can seem so insignificant and ordinary, but they are illuminated by a life-light, a love and a grace, a hope and a way that is so deep and true it connects our very depths to the very depths of a God who loves us enough to come, in fragile flesh, and stretch out his arms to show us the full extent of his love. It is in our very ordinariness, our very smallness and failure and seeming insignificance, that we encounter the love and grace of God. Even there, we can live out of that life-light. We can live in abundant life.

Reflection and response

Study

John 18:1–11

- How do you respond to the arrest taking place in a garden? Does this call to mind any other gardens?
- What do you think of the way Jesus steps forward to meet this large force? Would you say this feels like an act of non-violent resistance? How would you describe it?
- What is your response to situations where people stand up to protect others or stand up against injustice?
- Why might the soldiers have fallen to the ground – and then continue to arrest him?
- Do you agree that this passage enacts some of the meaning of the cross, as Jesus steps forward to save his friends?
- Do you feel Peter's action was justified?
- What do you understand by the talk of 'cup'? Could it relate to the cups of the Passover meal?

Further study

John 17:25—18:11; 18:15–27; 21:15–19

- Do you agree that there are echoes and patterns that emerge in these three passages? If so, why?
- How do you feel about Peter's treatment of Jesus, and Jesus' response?
- You might also like to look at the arrest in other gospels: Matthew 26:46–56; Mark 14:42–52; Luke 22:46–52.

Prayer and meditation

Dear God, may we be forever caught up in your love and life. May we never consider ourselves to be too small, too ordinary, too insignificant to be part of your great story of love and abundant life. May we remember how Jesus came, humbly, and compared himself to bread, to a shepherd, to a vine. May we see in the rough materials of our lives the wonder of your grace, your glory, your love. Amen

Creative response

Read through the three passages under 'Further study', paying attention to sources of light and darkness.

- How does the presence and absence of light affect the people in the narrative?
- Imagine yourself entering the scenes, one by one. What is the quality of light and heat? What do the shadows do? What is the purpose of the light/fire in each case? Then, compare the three. What strikes you?
- What fire might Jesus be kindling in you? To what purpose?

You might like to write a response or use colour to draw or paint it.

Life and service

> We can do no great things, only small things with great love.
> Mother Teresa of Calcutta[35]

As you consider the ordinariness and extraordinariness of 'I am', that great union of the everyday with the divine, develop the discipline of seeing each thing as capable of being filled with great love. This day, seek to do one humble thing with great love. Repeat every day.

Further reading

soulfood.me – a Church of England website

Notes

1 Elizabeth Barrett Browning, 'Aurora Leigh', *The Oxford Book of English Mystical Verse* (Nicholson and Lee, 1917).
2 Laurence Singlehurst, *Sowing, Reaping, Keeping* (InterVarsity Press, 2006).
3 William Wordsworth, 'The world is too much with us', *The New Oxford Book of English Verse* (Oxford University Press, 1972), p. 507.
4 George Herbert, 'Prayer' in *The New Oxford Book of English Verse* (Oxford University Press, 1972), p. 255.
5 Barbara Glasson, *I Am Somewhere Else* (Darton, Longman & Todd, 2006).
6 C.D. Younge, *The Works of Philo* (Hendrickson, 2005).
7 Andrea Skevington, *Prayers and Verses through the Bible* (Lion, 2016), p. 90.
8 Dietrich Bonhoeffer, *The Cost of Discipleship* (SCM Press, 2015).
9 This section is influenced by Barbara Brown Taylor, *Learning to Walk in the Dark: Because God often shows up at night* (Canterbury Press, 2015).
10 This phrase comes from St John of the Cross, *The Dark Night of the Soul* (Whitaker House, 2017).
11 A. Spearing (ed.), *The Cloud of Unknowing* (Penguin, 2001).
12 Kent Dobson (ed.), *First-Century Study Bible* (Zondervan, 2014), notes on Genesis 2:7; see also **newlife.id.au/equality-and-gender-issues/human-man-woman-genesis-2**.
13 Madeleine L'Engle, *Walking on Water: Reflections on faith and art* (Convergent Books, 2016), pp. 140–41.
14 Drawn from Rex Ambler, *Light to Live By: An exploration in Quaker spirituality* (Quaker Books, 2002).
15 Emily Dickinson, *The Complete Poems* (Faber and Faber, 1970), p. 666.
16 Gabriele Finaldi, *The Image of the Christ: Seeing salvation* (National Gallery, 2000), p. 12.
17 Thomas Merton, *Thoughts in Solitude* (Burns & Oates, 1975).
18 Julian of Norwich, *Revelations of Divine Love* (Penguin, 1998), p. 103.
19 For example, her canticle 'O noblissima viriditas'.

20 Wendell Berry, 'Manifesto: the mad farmer liberation front', *Reclaiming Politics* (Fall/Winter 1991), p. 62.
21 Shane Claibourne, *The Irresistible Revolution: Living as an ordinary radical* (Zondervan, 2006).
22 See **andreaskevington.com/2016/05/25/the-mary-at-your-feet-poems-three**.
23 A good starting point is sections 16–19 of Julian of Norwich, *Revelations of Divine Love* (Penguin, 1998), pp. 64–70.
24 From Rob Bell, *Velvet Elvis* (Zondervan, 2005), p. 130.
25 As attributed in Kelly S. Johnson, *The Fear of Beggars: Stewardship and poverty in Christian ethics* (Eerdmans, 2007), p. 209.
26 Quoted in a sermon at St Edmundsbury Cathedral.
27 Wendell Berry, 'The peace of wild things' in Neil Astley (ed.), *Being Alive* (Bloodaxe Books, 2004), p. 72.
28 George Herbert, 'Love (III)' in *The New Oxford Book of English Verse* (Oxford University Press, 1972), p. 262.
29 Rachel Hickson, *Supernatural Communication* (New Wine Press, 2006), p. 93.
30 Richard Rohr, *The Divine Dance* (SPCK, 2016), p. 30.
31 See **en.wikipedia.org/wiki/Perichoresis**.
32 Josephus, *Jewish War* (Penguin, 1985), vv. 210–12.
33 Hudson Taylor, quoted in Watchman Nee, *The Normal Christian Life* (Bottom of the Hill Publishing, 2014), pp. 56–57.
34 The original is found in *Carmina Gadelica* (Floris Books, 1992), adapted by Cecil F. Alexander, 1889.
35 Common translation/paraphrase. 'Don't look for big things, just do small things with great love' from Brian Kolodiejchuk (ed.), *Mother Teresa, Come Be My Light* (Image, 2009).